SEEDS, SPADES, HEARTHS, AND HERDS

The Domestication of Animals and Foodstuffs

SEEDS, SPADES, HEARTHS, AND HERDS

The Domestication of Animals and Foodstuffs

SECOND EDITION

CARL O. SAUER

The MIT Press
Cambridge, Massachusetts, and London, England

Foreword to the First Edition

The Isaiah Bowman Memorial Fund was established by Mr. Archer M. Huntington as a permanent trust, the income to be used for such purposes as the Council of the Society may deem most fitting. At the meeting of the Council held on February 15, 1950, it was decided to apply the greater part to the institution of a series of lectures to be delivered at intervals by distinguished scholars on subjects to be chosen from the wide range of Dr. Bowman's interests.

The first of the series, "Geography, Justice, and Politics at the Paris Conference of 1919," given in 1951, by Charles Seymour, President Emeritus of Yale University, reflected Dr. Bowman's concern with political man and his world. The second series was given by Carl O. Sauer, Chairman of the Department of Geography, University of California, Berkeley, in the Harkness Theatre of Columbia University, New York City, on January 29 and 30 and February 1, 4, and 6, 1952. It reflects an aspect of Dr. Bowman's interest in pioneer man—in this instance, literally the pioneer of a new world. Not only in theme but in approach does it reveal the fresh, inquiring spirit of the pioneer. Such a lecture series as this primarily looks to the far horizons. As Professor Sauer himself expresses it: A senior scholar reviews the status of knowledge in a field of his major interest and sketches the frontiers on which he sees good prospects of new learning. He does not try to give a well-polished abstract of accepted learning, as much as a prospectus of that which is not securely within our grasp.

[v]

Foreword to the Second Edition

The articles reprinted here are pieces of a long-developing interest in the remote course of human activity, in which, here and there, unnamed peoples turned to keeping and breeding plants and animals for whatever purposes. We call this act or series of acts domestication, a word that implies attachment to the household and management to meet domestic wants. This taking of particular plants and animals under human care and modification had as result what has been called the Neolithic agricultural revolution, which I have come to doubt more and more as begun because of increased population and diminished supply of food. Nor do I regard it as a general stage of economic and social evolution denied only to the inhabitants of adverse environments, but think of it as a cultural advance achieved only where people of special inclinations and of leisure gave peculiar and sustained attention to the care and propagation of certain plants and animals. This is the major theme I have tried to develop.

Indians of Sonora, Papagos, Opatas, and Mayos gave me the first lessons not only in what they grew, the common threesome of corn, beans, and squash, but also in varieties particular to those parts and retained from the prehistoric past, as were their ways of storage. Thus began a learning that cultivated plants are living artifacts of times past, available where archeology and written document are wanting, or making these more explicit.

Observations, including those of Spaniards who had come early, and a little archeology gradually fitted into a geographic pattern of the New World that appeared to show two major regions of plant and animal domestication. In the northern one crops were grown for their harvest of seeds by the planting and selection of seeds. From the Caribbean south, the dominant procedure was vegetative reproduction, planting pieces of stalks or roots; also there was more domestication of animals. The seed complex penetrated south to a greater extent than the other moved north. Thus the question, Did the two systems develop independently or is one derived from the other? The theme is reconsidered in two articles appended to the main text of earlier date. The third appended essay poses the question of dispersal into the Old World of maize, the Indian corn.

Lacking a proper inclusive term I have used the word agriculture as admitting animal husbandry without commitment to kind of animal or manner of tillage. The restrictive distinctions between agriculture and horticulture (the latter often used for American Indians) also seem unnecessary or improper. For the most part those who cultivated plants also kept animals.

By an old and still persisting view, cultural innovation has been held to have been by stages, beginning with collecting, followed by hunting. Hunters became herdsmen, and sedentary living with the cultivation of crops came later. The stage theory was strongly challenged by Eduard Hahn at the end of the past century; he held that plant and animal domestication was carried out by the same people, who were sedentary villagers. In his view the mobile herdsmen were late offshoots of agricultural people who migrated into steppes and deserts and turned exclusively to herding.

The theory of a general succession of stages rests on the inferred need of growing populations for increased supply of food. Hahn opposed such economic motivation, especially for domestic animals, and proposed their introduction in religious ceremonies. More on this in the text. It holds good for the New World, to my knowledge, and may be valid in the Old. A large extension of known time has been added to civilizations in the Near East, village- and town-dwelling people, who grew crops and kept animals. In particular the excavations by Kathleen Kenyon at Jericho and by James Mellaart at Çatal Hüyük, the latter on the Anatolian Plateau north of the Taurus Mountains, are giving a surprisingly elaborate picture of sedentary life reaching back around ten thousand years.*

In the New World the cultivation of certain plants, including squash and beans, has been determined to about nine thousand years before the present (Richard MacNeish, Tehuacan, Puebla, Mexico; and Kent Flannery, State of Oaxaca, Mexico). There is no early record of domestic animals here; maize came later, as did bread wheat in the Near East.

In both Old and New World cultivated plants, selected and modified by man, were grown long before pottery was made. Baskets, wooden vessels, pits, and perhaps gourds provided the earlier containers for storage and cooking. The first potters perhaps coiled rolls of clay in the manner of baskets made by coils of fiber plants. The digging stick of the ancient collectors became the planting implement of the cultivators — the primitive pointed spade used to thrust into the ground. The hoe is poorly suited to primitive breaking

---

*James Mellaart, *Çatal Hüyük* (1967), with introduction by Sir Mortimer Wheeler, includes an overview of other parts of the Near East.

of ground. *It might serve to heap up loose earth but a transversely hafted blade of wood, bone, shell, or stone is a poor instrument to penetrate the ground compared to the thrust of the planting stick, in effect a heavy wooden spear. It is now apparent that cultivation was carried on in the Old World for a long time before there was plow agriculture. In the New World forms of the planting stick, such as the Mexican* coa, *continued to be the basic implement. The distinguishing style of cultivation in the New World is that whatever was to be grown, whether seed, root, or cutting, was placed by hand in mounds of earth or into prepared ridges, not broadcast.*

With these preliminary and qualifying remarks the topic of agricultural origins and dispersals is presented in the several forms I have considered in the past years.

Contents

Agricultural Origins and Dispersals

I

Man — Ecologic Dominant

On Time as a Dimension of Geography

The focused curiosity that bears the name "geography" is or should be aware not only of the dependence of life on the physical environment, but also of the interdependence of living things in a common habitat, or of total ecology. The complete geographer must always be learning about the skills that men employ and about the objects, living and inanimate—total environment—to which such skills are applied. He is interested in discovering related and different patterns of living as they are found over the world—culture areas. These patterns have interest and meaning as we learn how they came into being. The geographer, therefore, properly is engaged in charting the distribution over the earth of the arts and artifacts of man, to learn whence they came and how they spread, what their contexts are in cultural and physical environments.

We are dealing in large part with observations of the present that originated in a past which does not come again, or which cannot be verified experimentally. We may, in fact, both as to nature and culture, be making reconstructions of past scenes and acts greatly different from what is now. We use the testimony of eye witnesses if we can find such, and also whatever circumstantial evidence that can be brought to bear on the reconstruction. Time, changing in tempo and usually non-recurrent as to mode, spreads a veil we can never fully lift. Yet, if we are trying to learn about the changing, man-inhabited world, human geography must take the risks of interpreting the meeting of natural history and cultural history and that, perhaps, is as much of a definition as we need. Our problems have four dimensions and we cannot simplify them by, or as, academic abstractions.

I like that expression, the meeting of natural and cultural history, partly because I prefer natural history with its sense of real, non-duplicated time and place to ecology, and culture history for the same reason to sociology or social science. The things with which we are concerned are changing continuously and without end, and they take place, for good reason, not anywhere, but somewhere, that is in actual situations or places. That succession of events with which we deal is quite other than the conceptual models that are set up as regular, recurrent, or parallel stages and cycles. Such have been much liked by students both of plant and human ecology. Among geographers, William Morris Davis delayed somewhat our learning about the physical earth by his systems of attractive but unreal cycles of erosion, with their stages of youth, maturity, old age, and rejuvenation. Plant ecology also has been affected by Davisian views. Such concepts are sometimes, but improperly, called "evolutionistic." Actually, evolution operates by continuing variation and divergence. It does not return to a previous condition, and rarely rests. I shall—on several occasions—argue against parallel recurrence and for accumulating divergences.

Man alone ate of the fruit of the Tree of Knowledge and thereby began to acquire and transmit learning, or "culture." With each new skill he found in his surroundings more opportunity, or "resources," to fashion products of use to himself, to improve his well-being, and to increase his numbers. An environment can only be described in terms of the knowledge and preferences of the occupying persons: "natural resources"

[2]

are in fact cultural appraisals. Occasionally, a new idea arose in some group and became a skill and institution. Such innovation might bring out new possibilities of the homeland; it might also give competitive advantage over neighboring folk, and set in motion pressures eased by migration.

There is no general law of progress that all mankind follows; there are no general successions of learning, no stages of culture, through which all people tend to pass. There have been progressive cultures and others that show almost no signs of change. The latter are to be found in areas of high isolation; the former have been favored by the nature and location of their homelands. The parallel to biologic evolution is significant. Invention begins by small increments of insight, variant ideas that gain acceptance under a favorable cultural climate. Variation follows on variation and may build up into a significantly new way and view of life. Now and then, in a few and, I may repeat, physically favored areas some such center has burst forth into a great period of significant invention, from which ideas spread, and in part changed as they spread afield. These centers of major and sustained innovation were always few. In the history of man, unless I misread it greatly, diffusion of ideas from a few hearths has been the rule; independent, parallel invention the exception. The identification of such creative culture hearths is the topic of this discourse, in terms of the domination by man of other organisms.

As artificer of cultural change, man has become increasingly powerful in modifying the plant and animal world surrounding him. The history of mankind is a long and diverse series of steps by which he has achieved ecologic dominance. He has intervened, with and without design, to increase and decrease, to expel or exterminate and to introduce, to modify and even to originate organic entities. Largely he has prospered by disturbing the natural order. Often, however, he overreaches himself and the new order he has introduced may end in disaster. As man became civilized he has grown more and more inclined to consider the earth as made for him to inherit, himself as the claimant of an anthropocentric order; he has come to believe in an ever-expanding system that places no limits upon himself other than his individual mortality. Often his capacity to know good from evil has been warped by the energy of his activities, his knowledge giving him powers which he has lacked the wisdom to control. Our own time has its prophets of progress unlimited in numerous social and physical scientists who speak of remaking the world. It may be proper, at this time of dizzy cultural change, to regard our past record as modifiers of the organic world.

A Personal Note

My own experiences have been almost wholly with the New World. By chance and choice I have turned away from commercialized areas and dominant civilizations to conservative and primitive areas. I have found pleasure in "backward" lands, where the demands of industry for materials and markets are little felt. In terms of the ever unsatisfied world economy these are the "underdeveloped areas" that are to be made over and thereby to lose their own ways and values. It is to these, thus far happily undisturbed places, that recollection turns, under whatever skies they lie, for a comparative reading of cultural processes and contexts elsewhere and of other times.

My first field season, of 1910, was in the Upper Illinois Valley. Some of these early observations raised questions that have come back elsewhere again and again to occupy my mind. The upland mantle of loess introduced me to the problems of Ice-Age climates. The prairies that extended across the uplands to the margins of the valleys posed the question of grassland ecology. Indian fields and those of the pioneer whites, always situated within the woodlands, started an interest in the nature of primitive cultivation. What I wrote then about industrial location and such matters I have long since forgotten, but as to these three items, that valley of forty years ago is still green in my memory. They were the starting point from which trails have led in later years into different and distant parts.

The Primordial Habitat

As to the primordial home and nature of man we have a few clues. He is less specialized in his physiology than the apes; in particular he is able to eat a wide range of foods, suggesting that a great diversity was available to him. This wide feeding capacity predisposed him to experiment with different foodstuffs. Neither heavy forest nor open grassland was suited to his earliest state. A peculiarly long and helpless infancy argues against the view that our kind began as roving bands. His water needs are high and frequent, requiring certain cultural skills before he could penetrate lands of drought.

The earliest homes of our kind are to be sought in tempered climes, not heavily forested, places either on the outer margins of the tropics or elevated above the rain forests. Such mesothermal climates have opposed rainy and dry seasons, with growing and resting periods of vegetation, and with times of greater and less abundance of food. Our ancestors may therefore not have begun as improvident fellows, alternating between feast and famine. Storing food in times of plenty against a time of want may be an original human trait, as it is for many animals. The cradle of our race may well have lain in what would still seem to us pleasant places, of mild weather with alternating rainy and dry seasons, of varied woodland, shrub and herbs, a land of hills and valleys, of streams and springs, with alluvial reaches and rock shelters in cliffs. Our place of origin was one of invitation to the well-being of our kind.[1]

Ice-Age Climates and the Spread of Man

If we are now living in an interglacial stage, as seems likely, the whole documented span of human existence falls within the Ice Age. Never, in so far as we know, has the earth undergone more extreme and recurrent climatic changes. The old concept of Ice-Age weather based upon the simple equation of low temperatures and glaciation, rising temperatures and deglaciation, is now being replaced by an adequate dynamic interpretation.[2] When the general circulation of the atmosphere produced large north-south exchanges of air masses, ice caps formed in high latitudes through the poleward thrust of moist, mild air, along with greater cloud cover. At such times, pluvial conditions seem to have prevailed over some of the present arid lands. Sea level was generally lowered by several hundred feet by the locking up of water in ice caps. During the major deglaciations, the world climates may well have resembled our present pattern, with great winter cold in high latitudes, with wide deserts of drought, and with high sea levels. Man's occupation spread and ebbed with these physical changes, but not similarly the overall habitability of the earth.

The earliest known human records attest man's possession of fire. He could live in wintry lands, therefore, if he could supply himself with food. Very early in Pleistocene time, man was living widely over the Old World, inhabiting England, Morocco, South Africa, Java, and probably North China.[3] The ice and snowbound lands of the far north, however, exacted skills beyond the attainments of primitive man. The tundras are still about the emptiest lands as to human population, and the subarctic lands of fir, spruce, and muskeg are still difficult.

The food resources of the far north are mainly aquatic and at the water margins, and may be cut off in winter. Only folk of quite advanced hunting, fishing, and storage skills can live there, specialists in survival in a most difficult environment. Primitive, artless man had no chances there.

Thereby we come to the entry of man into the New World. The conventional view allows him only a few thousand years over here; it developed in the '90's at a time when man (*Homo sapiens*) was considered as of late origin in the Old World, more or less near the end of the last glaciation. Human time has been expanded steadily for the Old World, but hardly revised at all for the New. An occasional geographer has protested as did Albrecht Penck in 1928 and George Carter in 1951.[4]

If man first came to America only ten or twenty thousand years ago, as tradition holds, northern Asia and North America, through which the passage took place, differed little in climate from the present, though there were larger ice masses. Really primitive folk could never have made the crossing as they could not make it now. I do not see that anything less than the specialized hunting, fishing, and cold-adaptive skills of such late comers as Eskimos and Athabaskans could have made human life possible across the far north. Yet both North and South America have held many tribes of very rudimentary arts, for whom there is no indication that they ever possessed such skills.

At much earlier times there were greatly different and genial climates in high latitudes. At times during the Pleistocene, important migrations took place of non-boreal animals, such as horses and camels going from the New World to the Old, elephants and bovines in the opposite direction. Among later immigrants from the Old World were mammoths and the

[7]

immediate ancestors of our bison and deer. All such dispersals were by land across the Bering Strait during a milder climate and lower sea level. The best time after the early Pleistocene for movement between the Old and New Worlds seems to have been during the Third (Illinoian) glaciation.[5] Then the lands bordering the North Pacific were freely supplied with moist, warm air from the ocean to the south and, though mountain snows were breeding glaciers, the lowlands should have remained warmed and free from permanently frozen ground. With a dropping sea level that formed a land bridge at and south of Bering Strait, the streams, Alaskan and Siberian, flowing across the lowlands also cut down their valleys. The land was well drained; in place of ice and waterlogged plains rolling lowlands may have reached to the present Arctic coast. Instead of tundra and muskeg there were mixed woodlands including white birch, willow, alder, and poplar. Some of the streams may well have remained open in winter. At such time, man could make his entry into the New World as readily as did the other mammals which were not denizens of boreal climates. He had them to prey upon; he had plants that were useful and familiar, and wood aplenty for fire and shelter. Later, but perhaps well back in Wisconsin time the weather hardened, permafrost and tundra spread, flora and fauna were impoverished to Arctic levels.

Convention has chosen the most unlikely time for our first settlers. The optimal time, it has been suggested, of genial weather, varied biota, and low sea level would have been during the development of the Illinoian glaciation. Thus, about a third way back through the Ice Age the same invitation to pass at leisure through an easy gateway was available to animals, plants, and man. Well before this time man had become dis-

tributed to pretty far ends of Old World continents. No reason
has been offered as to why he should not have gone where went
bear, bison, and deer, and I see no reason why he should not
have availed himself of the same favorable opportunity to colonize the New World.

Early Rate of Culture Growth

The remains of man have been traced back at least to the
conventional beginning of the Pleistocene; his biologically inferred origins are much older. We still lack a proper yardstick
for glacial time, but for the present may use the old estimate of
a million years, this scale being quite satisfactory for plant and
animal evolution, and also for the weathering and sculpture of
the land that has taken place.

The preserved tools of Ice-Age man for a very long time
were rude and of little diversity. Innovation and regional spe-
cialization became more marked in the second half of the Ice
Age, and notable in the Upper Paleolithic of Europe, which
occupied most of the fourth or last glacial stage. The explanation of the low rate of culture growth for most (nine-tenths or
more?) of human time does not need to be sought in his physical evolution, since the old views of the lateness and separate-
ness of *Homo sapiens* have broken down. It was not his brain
that held ancient man back; it was the little he had to think
about for so long. Ideas must build upon ideas and such accumulation and derivation, culture growth, that is, appears to
have been very slow for a very long time. The distribution of
nearly identical Paleolithic artifacts over very large areas also
suggests that local centers of divergence — different kinds of
ideas expressed in different practical applications — were rare.
However, since the record is almost solely in worked stone, it

may be poorly representative; almost only the ideas that were expressed in one kind of durable but refractory material have been preserved.

Fire as a Culture Trait

Through all ages the use of fire has perhaps been the most important skill to which man has applied his mind. Fire gave to man, a diurnal creature, security by night from other predators. Hearth and home are still synonymous. About the fireside the last duties of the day are done, the events of the day reviewed and the morrow planned. The fireside was the beginning of social living, the place of communication and reflection.

Feeding the fire, man learned wood working, how to point a shaft, hollow out a vessel, and thus later to make a boat. Above all, fire provided ways of experimenting with food. Man digests raw starch and plant proteins poorly. Knowing how to cook, even the most primitive people have explored largely the food possibilities of roots, stems, buds, and fruits within their reach. Even food resources that require careful processing by heat or leaching, or both, in order not to make ill or to kill, have not been overlooked. These are the beginnings of scientific observation. Such knowledge is botany, by the precise identification of plant entities, and chemistry, by repeating properly the successful experiment.

Cooking by dry or moist heat long preceded boiling. Hearths on top of the ground and cooking pits dug into the ground are both very ancient, the former for roasting, baking, and broiling, the latter for pit steaming over a bed of coals. From Cape Cod to Chiloé the natives knew the "clambake," a complete meal by pit steaming of fish, flesh, greens, and tubers. In the island of Chiloé, for instance, a pit is dug in the sandy shore; over a bed of coals a layer of kelp is spread, then layers of shell-fish, fish, potatoes (formerly oxalis tubers and lileaceous bulbs), leaves for cooked greens, and finally a cover of kelp. The result is a complete and savory meal. The Indians of the tip of Lower California, about as primitive as any in the Americas, roasted and baked tubers in ashes, parched and popped seeds in hot sand, and pit-steamed large quantities of turgid mescal (agave) flower-stalk buds. The basic techniques of cooking are immemorially older than pots, kettles, or even water-holding baskets.

Fuel always is in major demand. Through the ages man has moved more ton-miles of fuel than of any other commodity, whatever his cultural level. Where he lived on seacoasts and river banks his stock of driftwood might be replenished perennially. Elsewhere, man found in time that his fuel consumption exceeded the natural rate of supply, which was mainly dead stuff fallen to the ground. Also, he was, early, a user of bark and bast and thus came to know that a tree with its phloem destroyed, died. He acquired therefore the basic knowledge necessary for keeping up his wood supplies and also for clearing ground by deadening trees rather than by felling them. As professional camper, he chose his camp first by water, next by the available fuel.

Fire was much used in getting food, and some peoples learned how to set fires so as to improve plant reproduction along desired lines for the seasons ahead. I know of no American aborigines who did not set fires for hunting or collecting purposes at suitable seasons, if they lived where the vegetation was inflammable. Fires were set to smother small animals, to drive larger ones to a place convenient for the kill, to clear the ground for easier collecting of seeds, nuts, and acorns.[6] Even the obtuse Tasmanians helped their food gathering by burning over the ground. A little-explored subject is the use of fire to change the character of the vegetation deliberately, as to provide browse for deer or to stimulate the growth of freely seeding useful annuals. In not a few cases, fire became a deliberate instrument of land management by deliberate deformation of the plant association.

We need not think of ancestral man as living in vagrant bands, endlessly and unhappily drifting about. Rather, they were as sedentary as they could be and set up housekeeping at one spot for as long as they might. In terms of the economist, our kind has always aimed at minimizing assembly costs. The first principle of settlement geography is that the group chose its living site where water and shelter were at hand, and about which food, fuel, and other primary needs could be collected within a convenient radius. Relocation came when it was apparent that some other spot required less effort, as with seasonal changes in supplies. Consumer goods were brought to the hearth and processed there. Women were the keepers of the fire, and there prepared the food and cared for the children. They were the ones most loath to move, the home makers and accumulators of goods. The early hearths recovered by archeology are not casual camps, but fire places used so long and sites so significantly altered as to have withstood the obliterating effects of time. The normal primitive geographic pattern is that of a community, a biologic and social group, clustering about hearths at the points of least transport, holding a collecting territory for its exclusive use, and relocating itself as infrequently as necessary.

Fire as an Ecologic Agent

In Genesis it is said that man was given dominion over every living thing. From the first he asserted himself as ecologic dominant. He lived confidently, not in fear. At first a lesser predator, he became chief among them, crowding back the animals that competed with him for food. Being omnivorous, he became numerous in areas of attraction; acquiring more skills he made more and more plants and animals dependent on his suffrance or favor.[7]

His greatest power to disturb the balance of nature lay in his employment of fire. He used it for certain ends, the effects went much farther. Collectors, hunters, tillers, and pastoral folk, set fires; civilized man alone is interested in suppressing them. The haze of Indian summer has the smell of smoke proper to it. The non-commercial landscapes of Latin America still are blurred toward the end of any dry season by a haze of smoke that lingers until the rains set in.

Burning is ineffective at the climatic extremes. Where the surface of the ground remains moist, litter does not ignite and fire cannot spread. However, many tropical forest floors become dry enough at times to be burnable. High latitudes may be protected by high ground moisture and low evaporation. Deserts have their plants too widely spaced and accumulate too little litter for burning. Semiarid lands of lower latitudes may be resistant to burning. The scrub savannas of western Mexico are well stocked with woody growth, especially with leguminous shrubs of small, divided leaves. These stay in leaf for several months, gradually defoliating during the dry season. The leaflets drop bit by bit and soon break up. There is no formation of a continuous litter and no chance for fire to run over the surface.

Little is known of the effectiveness of natural fires. Natural burning occurs with rainless lightning, or with light rain and thunderstorms following on a pronounced dry period. In our western mountains, especially at high elevations, lightning-set fires are common. Whether they affect the same spots sufficiently often to maintain a fire-altered vegetation, I do not know; the subject invites study.

The great fires that we have come to fear are effects of our civilization. These are the crown fires of great depth and heat, notorious aftermaths of the pyres of slash left by lumbering. We also increase fire hazard by the very giving of fire protection which permits the indefinite accumulation of inflammable litter. Under the natural and primitive order, such holocausts, that leave a barren waste, even to the destruction of the organic soil, were not common. Rather, these were low ground fires burning lightly over the surface, searing the young growth to a height of a very few feet and consuming the dry trash but not affecting the actual soil.

All fires alter plant reproduction; the more so, the longer and more often they recur. Plants that are favored by burning have been called pyrophytes. The Berkeley, Calif., fire of 1923 gave an extreme test of survival. Most shrubs and trees were killed, with the exception of palms and dracaenas and some pines and redwoods. The former survived because, as woody monocotyledons, they were not dependent on external growth tissue. Thus palms, singly and in clumps, accent the fire-swept savannas of tropical lands as do the Cordylines the tussock plains of New Zealand. Redwoods, numerous pines, and some oaks are insulated by thick corky bark that burns poorly and conducts heat poorly. Some pine forests, as of our eastern and western yellow pines, may be in part the result of burning.

The long-lived trees and shrubs die out gradually under recurrent burning because their progeny is destroyed. The number of mature and maturing trees and shrubs grows less in time; the woods grow more and more open and toward the last are park lands, the last guard of mature trees, without issue. In the run of centuries, the slowly maturing woody plants that reproduce by seed disappear, if fires are more frequent than the time needed for seedlings to outgrow the fire-sensitive stage. More and more the vegetation shifts to plants that reproduce from protected rootstocks and underground stems and to the freely-seeding annuals and plurannuals. The plant cover may become entirely herbaceous.[8]

Grassland Climax

The young science of ecology has undertaken to study the associations of organisms, initially as belonging together by their physiologic requirements or their joint adaptation to a particular physical environment. Systems of classification arose that identified plant and animal complexes with climate. Thus there arose the concept of the "ecologic climax," currently defined as "the final or stable type of plant community reached in a particular climate." A postulate tends to displace reality. Climatic regions are cartographic abstractions, useful as elementary teaching devices to give some first notions of weather contrasts over the earth. "Final or stable" communities are quite exceptional in nature: weather, soils, and surfaces are continually changing; new organisms are immigrating or forming, old ones may be giving way. Change is the order of nature: climax assumes the end of change.

Since there are many grasslands about the world, such associations have been inferred to represent a grassland climax, that is, to be stable and the result of particular climates. The theme song became that every single grassland must have a climate for its own. When I had ecologic instruction with the admirable Cowles at Chicago, I was at first persuaded. More and more I had to admit that I was unable to find the coincidence of grassland and limiting values of moisture. Why should heavy-rooted woody plants be excluded from certain areas and these surrendered to the exclusive occupation by herbs and grasses? Thus I began to surmise that the plant ecologists had construed away the role of animals and especially of man.

I grew up in the timbered upland peninsula formed by the junction of the Missouri and Mississippi rivers. The prairie began a few miles to the north and extended far into Iowa. The broad rolling uplands were prairie, whatever their age and origin, the stream-cut slopes below them were timbered; river and creek valleys and flanking ridges were tree covered, be they formed in bed rock or on deep loess mantle. From grandparents I heard of the early days when people dared not build their houses beyond the shelter of the wooded slopes, until the plow stopped the autumnal prairie fires. In later field work in Illinois, in the Ozarks, in Kentucky, I met parallel conditions of vegetation limits coincident with break in relief. I gave up the search for climatic explanation of the humid prairies.

The Far West, of subhumid and semiarid climates, showed again the same relation of grassland to topography. The grassy valley basins of California, bordered by oak parks of senescent, non-reproducing trees,[9] the high plains of Arizona, New Mexico, Chihuahua, and Durango all are or had been grasslands lapped against rough, woody country lying above or below the plains. In the Latin-American vernacular, *monte* (mountain) has come to mean brush or woodland. Last, I became acquainted with tropical savannas in Central and South America, plains often studded with tall palms, with gallery forests along the valleys and with woody growth wherever there is broken terrain. Parts are semiarid, parts get as much rain as any part of the Mississippi Valley. Cattle grazers still keep up the aboriginal burning practice.

Such, in brief, has been the sum of my experience: Grasslands occupy plains; woody growth dominates rough terrain.

It does not follow, of course, that plains must be grassy, though grasslands and pine woods do characterize a lot of them. Fires sweep most freely over smooth surfaces, spreading before the wind until they are stopped at the brink of valleys cut below, or die out in hill and mountain lands that rise above them.

Grasslands shrink where protected from fire. The woods margin may advance by shading out the grasses. Animals and wind carry seeds, some of which grow where accidental openings occur in the herbaceous cover, and these accidents do happen. In the Kentucky Barrens or Pennyroyal[10] a gently undulating limestone upland of high fertility is surrounded by stream-cut terrain, the latter, at settlement, a forest of mixed hardwoods, the former a grassland, whence its name, Barrens. The Pennyroyal a century ago was noted by the gifted geologist David Dale Owen as having self-seeded woodlots in former grassland. These were enclosures fenced off to serve as stock pens. Owen attributed the grassland to fires, as by Indian burning, the woodlots to protection by white farmers. Aided by grazing stock, there has been under way lately an explosive advance of leguminous scrub, mesquite, catclaw, huisache, over former grasslands in northern Mexico and the Southwest. On the Staked Plains of Texas there has been wide invasion by dwarf white oak brush, on the southern Colorado Plateau of sagebrush.

In the natural course a maximum depth of plant growth tends to develop on any site. Between ceiling and floor a maximal diversity of organisms is accommodated to the full utilization of moisture, light, minerals, and organic food. Grasslands are living zones greatly reduced in depth, above and below the ground; they are simplified morphologically, and usually reduced as to diversity. They are an impoverished assemblage, not a fully developed organic household or community.

Continued Deformation by Man

In very many parts of the world, Old and New, man has been on hand for so long and in such numbers that great deformation of the vegetation has resulted. We can then hardly speak of a natural balance without him, since man has been exerting sustained and selective pressures. Except at the climatic extremes, there may be no such thing as undisturbed or natural vegetation.

Man, nurtured in the woodlands, has been of old the enemy of trees. He has exploited them, destroyed them, rarely favored them. His simplest skills were adequate to overcome the tree, for which he needed no ax, only the immemorial arts of setting fire and stripping bark. In the wood and brush lands in which most of mankind has lived over most of its span, the woody cover was progressively thinned and the ground more and more fully exposed to sun and air. Sun-requiring herbaceous plants increased at the expense of shade-tolerant ones. As Professor Ames pointed out[11] our crop plants are heliophile, and he thought of the parental forms of our economic annuals as evolving along with man. Man also was an agent of plant evolution by carrying plants to new places, along his paths, to his dooryard, on the refuse heap. New variations arose by such carriage, both as hybrids and mutants, adapted to the new situations. About him, plants that tolerated the man-made environment and served his ends became dominant. Quantitative and qualitative changes in plant life were initiated by man's mastery of fire; they grew with every increase in his numbers and of his economy.

Planters of the Old World and Their Household Animals

Antecedents of Domestication

It took man so very long to get around to the invention of agriculture that we may well doubt that the idea came easily or that it came from hunger, as is often supposed. Archeology has traced Neolithic farming back in the Near East for seven to eight thousand years, a late date in the history of the human race. These earliest Neolithic farmers were far removed in time and place, as I shall argue, from the origins of agriculture. Their crops, animals, and in part even their houses were not very different from those now existing in the same areas; one is inclined to say that they were nearer to the contemporary than to the original agriculture, the beginnings of which may well lie several times seven thousand years in the past.

It may be noted that the earliest Neolithic farmers lived at the time when the sea had risen to about its present level, that is, when a rough balance had been struck between ice formation and ice melt. I have previously made the inference that world weather was then not greatly different from the present. Before this time, that is, during the last deglaciation, the major part of the basic inventions of agriculture must have been made.

There is little dissent from the view that agricultural arts were first developed in the Old World and such origin is here accepted. The place and manner of their beginnings are the topic next under consideration, a central and classical question in anthropogeography. Geographers together with biologists in the past have contributed evidence on the nature and origins of agriculture. Combined with the findings of archeology, a more adequate interpretation is now gradually taking form. The classical view, carried down from Roman authors, that mankind progresses on a general sequence of stages, beginning as collectors through hunting and pastoral nomadism to agriculture, is still current in serious writing. Humboldt made the first breach in this position by pointing out that the New World had advanced agricultures but no pastoral nomads. Ritter was impressed by the few favored foci in which progressive cultures arose and from which crops spread. Moriz Wagner originated a corollary to Darwin by the thesis that biologic variation arose through migration into a new environment. Ratzel formulated the principle of diffusion as dominant over parallel invention. Hahn based animal domestication on non-economic grounds. The anthropogeographers have been maligned as environmentalists; actually they have been least guilty of proposals that similar environments develop similar ways, and have been most critical of parallel inventions and of general succession of stages of culture.

My own observations on primitive agriculture have been gathered in various parts of the New World. I have used these as aids in thinking comparatively about what I have been able to read about the Old World. The evidence gathered from workers in various parts and different disciplines seems to me to indicate a revised interpretation as to how agriculture arose. This presentation will serve its purpose if it is an incentive to further examination of the problem. First, certain basic premises:

　　1) Agriculture did not originate from a growing or chronic

shortage of food. People living in the shadow of famine do not have the means or time to undertake the slow and leisurely experimental steps out of which a better and different food supply is to develop in a somewhat distant future. Famine foods, and there are a number that are so-called, seem to have little relation to the plants ennobled by cultivation. The improvement of plants by selection for better utility to man was accomplished only by a people who lived at a comfortable margin above the level of want. The saying that necessity is the mother of invention largely is not true. The needy and miserable societies are not inventive, for they lack the leisure for reflection, experimentation, and discussion.

2) The hearths of domestication are to be sought in areas of marked diversity of plants or animals, where there were varied and good raw materials to experiment with, or in other words, where there was a large reservoir of genes to be sorted out and recombined. This implies well-diversified terrain and perhaps also variety of climate.

3) Primitive cultivators could not establish themselves in large river valleys subject to lengthy floods and requiring protective dams, drainage, or irrigation. I was bothered by the thesis of the potamic origin of agriculture in the great valleys of the Near East until I had assurance from Vavilov, in a visit of a quarter of a century ago, that all the investigations of his group pointed to origins in hill and mountain lands.

4) Agriculture began in wooded lands. Primitive cultivators could readily open spaces for planting by deadening trees; they could not dig in sod or eradicate vigorous stoloniferous grasses. Indian farming, except for the most advanced cultures, remained woodland farming. Years ago I objected to the then general European view that the loess lands were the lands of Neolithic agriculture because they were grassy. I proposed that

they were colonized by early farmers because they were meso-phytic woodlands, easily dug and productive.[1] Lately, some European scholars have shifted to the view that farming began in woodlands.[2]

5) The inventors of agriculture had previously acquired special skills in other directions that predisposed them to agri-cultural experiments. Of all peoples those most given to hunt-ing were least apt to incline toward domestication and breed-ing of plants, or, I think, of animals. There are suggestions in Paleolithic archeology that not the workers of flakes and shapers of blades, that is, the hunters, but the ax users, inter-preted as woodland dwellers, were remote ancestors of the agriculturists.

6) Above all, the founders of agriculture were sedentary folk. I have already said that groups move as little as their needs of food, water, fuel, and shelter require. Mobility as a dominant character goes with specialized hunting economies or with life in meager environments. Growing crops require constant at-tention. I have never seen primitive plantings that are not closely watched over until the crop is secured. A planted clear-ing anywhere is a feast set for all manner of wild creatures that fly, walk, and crawl to come in and raid fruits, leaves, and roots. What is food for man is feast for beasts. And, therefore, by day and night some one must drive off the unbidden wild guests. Planting a field and then leaving it until the harvest would mean loss of harvest.[3]

The Progenitors

After the Upper Paleolithic hunters of big game in Europe, the Aurignacian, Solutrean, and Magdalenian folk, and before the early Neolithic farmers of the Near East and Europe, an intervening culture is being recovered by archeology. This

Mesolithic period differed largely from the preceding hunting ways, has been identified especially along the Mediterranean and in Atlantic Europe, and seems to have been immigrant into Europe from Asia and Africa. It used, and perhaps introduced the bow and arrow; it employed fishing gear, fishhooks and lines, nets and sinkers, boats and paddles, none of them known earlier; it had a new style of ax and adz, with chisel edge; toward the last there was crude pottery; especially, it brought the dog, unknown for the preceding hunters, but characteristic of Mesolithic settlements.

The main interests of this culture were not in hunting by land, but in living by sea, stream, and lake, depending on fishing and water-side hunting and collecting. These habits and the time of its coming are probably responsible for the meagerness of Mesolithic record. At that time, because the ice caps were melting away, sea levels were rising markedly, and hence rivers were filling their valley floors so that only chance locations not buried beneath sea or alluvium may be found. The known settlements may have derived from major cultural changes that took place far to the East as a western, marginal extension, a simplified frontier, frontiers being likely to carry a reduced and simplified form of the culture from which they spring. I lay weight especially on the appearance of the dog and the fishing arts. Europe, until late historic time, appears to have been always a far peninsula of the Old World, receiving belated and reduced ideas from east or south.

The progenitors of the earliest agriculturists I have sought in some well-situated, progressive fishing folk living in a mild climate along fresh waters. Fresh water is postulated rather than salt because seaside vegetation has contributed little and late to the making of crop plants. For sedentary living there must have been available a long season or year-round staple resource in fish and other aquatic life. Clustering of groups in permanent villages was made possible at sites continually advantageous for fishing, such as stream junctions, lake outlets, rapids. Waterways served as lines of communication with other villages and so for the exchange and growth of ideas. Waterfowl, riparian mammals, waterside plants gave diversity to food. Basts and fibers were used to make nets and lines and suitable woods were at hand for boats and paddles.

There seems to be a connection between fiber preparation and the taking of fish by use of plant extracts to stun or kill them. These stupefying substances, in Spanish *barbasco,* commonly are alkaloids, they often lather freely, and are likely to be taken from plants also used for cordage, making bark cloth, and as detergents. The latter uses may have come first, and through them, the discovery that fish were stunned when certain plants were macerated or retted in water, without affecting the food quality of the fish. In the Old World, this barbasco trait is most elaborated in Southeast Asia, whence it radiates outward through the Pacific Islands, westward through the Mediterranean to Atlantic Europe and southwestward through forest Africa. The procedure is sufficiently characteristic and complex that it may have a common origin. This curious way of fishing is apparently older than, and may be a forerunner of, agriculture.[4]

The Cradle of Agriculture

As the cradle of earliest agriculture, I have proposed Southeastern Asia. It meets the requirements of high physical and organic diversity, of mild climate with reversed monsoons giving abundant rainy and dry periods, of many waters inviting to fishing, of location at the hub of the Old World for communication by water or by land. No other area is equally well situated or equally well furnished for the rise of a fishing-farming culture. I shall attempt to show that farming culture in origin is tied to fishing in this area, that the earliest and most literally domestic animals originated here, and that this is the world's major center of planting techniques and of amelioration of plants by vegetative reproduction. I accept the familiar premise that man learned to plant before he grew crops by seeding.

Planting and Plant Selection

The creative curiosity of man in the monsoon lands has operated strongly with asexual plant reproduction. Multiplication and selection is from clones. A piece of a plant is set into the ground to make a new plant. This may be by an offset or sprout from the parent, by dividing a root stock, by a stem cutting, or by a piece of underground stem or tuber. An individual plant is divided and multiplied indefinitely. The thing grown is identical reconstitution of parent rather than variant progeny. Selection begins by choosing the individual plant to be divided in order to make a number of plants that are like the parent. Selection proceeds by observing and preserving desirable individual variation, as in propagating an attractive chance root or bud sport, or by noting an accidental self-sown hybrid that is then divided for planting. In the long course of time, this continuous attention to the individual plant, and inattention to its sexual seeds, has given rise to an extraordinary lot of forms that are completely dependent on man for their existence. Seeds being of no interest, many such cultivated plants have lost the capacity to bear viable seeds, some as sterile polyploids, some in other ways. This culture operates by a very specific and sustained idea of reproduction; break the continuity of this operation and the plant may be lost.

The list of such man-made plants, or cultigens, is large, with eastern India in first place as to origin. Botanically, it includes especially many and important monocotyledons: Southeast Asia is the original home of the bananas. Genetic studies lately have resolved the variations in the Asiatic bananas with the result that the old distinction between bananas and plantains must be abandoned. One cultigen line derives directly from *Musa balbisiana,* native from Behar up to the Himalayas, another from the Malayan *M. acuminata,* the third main line involves hybrids between the two.[5] The domesticated forms of the ginger family, such as turmeric, appear to be mainly Indian. Aroids, cultivated for root or stem, including especially the taro, which is probably Indian, form a major food source especially out through the island world. For the home of the greater yam (*Dioscorea alata*) Burkill favors the east side of the Bay of Bengal, for *D. esculenta,* Indochina.[6] A half-dozen species of cultivated yams, some of them carried to the farthest Pacific Islands, throw important light on cultural radiation from the Southeast Asiatic mainland. Certain palms, especially the sago palm, pandans, bamboos, and sugar cane, have been widely carried out of India and Indochina and greatly altered by man. Dicotyledons have yielded shrubs, vines, and trees, greatly changed by immeasurably long vegetative selection, such as the leguminous derris cultivated for fish poison and insecticide, the several breadfruits, the citrus fruits, and persimmons (ebony family). The majority of the plants that have been thus made over by man are at home in well-drained alluvial lands, a few are river swamp plants, and some are aquatic.

The basic cultivated food plants of monsoon Asia do not constitute a balanced diet. They are sources of carbohydrates, mainly of starch, but also of sugar. Plant fats and oils are very minor, and vegetable proteins mostly lacking. The people who made the asexual crop plants had no need to develop a bal-

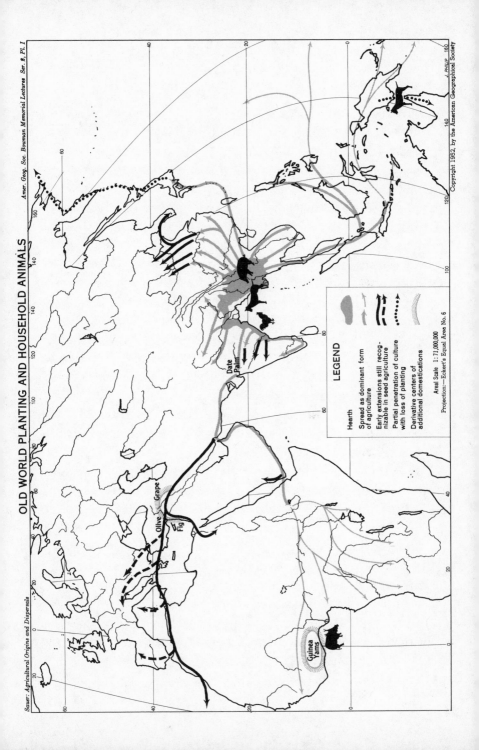

OLD WORLD PLANTING AND HOUSEHOLD ANIMALS

Amer. Geog. Soc. Bowman Memorial Lectures. Ser. 2, Pl. I

Sauer: Agricultural Origins and Dispersals

Copyright 1952, by the American Geographical Society

LEGEND

Hearth

Spread as dominant form of agriculture

Early extensions still recognizable in seed agriculture

Partial penetration of culture with loss of planting

Derivative centers of additional domestications

Areal Scale 1:71,000,000
Projection—Eckert's Equal Area No. 6

Date Palm

Olive
Grape
Fig

Guinea Yams

anced vegetarian diet, for they got their fats and proteins from animal food, originally fish and shell fish. The great preponderance and diversity of carbohydrate cultigens sustains the thesis that this was a fishing culture before it became a planting one. Other strong traits of this culture are the attention to the growing of spices—Southeast Asia included the spice lands of early commerce—and the emphasis on the coloring of food, person, and clothing, especially yellow or red (as by turmeric), with ceremonial significance attached thereto as life-giving, from birth through marriage to funerary offering.

These food plants may serve other purposes, especially as sources of fiber. Perhaps we have here another suggestion as to why fishermen began the cultivation and alteration of plants. Fiber, food, and ceremonial color may come from the same plant. *Cordyline fruticosa,* or *terminalis,* in such joint use among Malayans and Polynesians, is apparently of ancient introduction. Some of the pandans or screw pines have been widely carried by man and greatly selected by cutting propagation for matting, cordage, fruit, and scent. Breadfruits also have been a major source of barkcloth and of yellow dyes. It may well be that among the earliest domesticates were multi-purpose plants set out around fishing villages to provide starch food, substances for toughening nets and lines and making them water resistant, drugs, and poisons. Food production was one and perhaps not the most important reason for bringing plants under cultivation.

Plants that are grown from seed may be germinated before they are set out. Rice and coconut are familiar examples. Neither is considered to belong to the oldest planting culture. Rice probably originated in India; the place of origin of the coconut is still debated. Rice is the only cereal I know which is still a perennial, though in cultivation it is treated as an annual.

The custom of starting it in a seed bed and later setting the individual plants out cannot be explained entirely by the necessities of paddy cultivation and it is not so restricted. It has been suggested that rice was originally a weed in taro fields[7]; in weeding it was replanted elsewhere and a grain crop was produced, with partial retention of the vegetative planting habits. There is no necessity of starting coconuts in a seed bed and transplanting them later. Both customs suggest partial retention of the older idea of plant reproduction.

Plants of different kinds, growth habits, and uses were assembled in the same cultivated patches, not fields but simple gardens. The ground was dug with a planting stick, that later became spade or fork; the loosened ground often being mounded and the plants given added aeration and food by the heaping up of top soil.

Social Organization

In this culture the men built the boats and fished; the women had domain over the tilled land and the homes. Women were cooks and cultivators, domestics and domesticators. These societies were largely developed and organized by their women. It was through them, it is inferred, that descent was reckoned and membership in the household determined. Matrilineal and matriarchal societies arose. The *Kulturkreis* school seems to have a valid generalization in equating its "Old Planter" complex with matrilineal societies, and in linking to them multifamily houses, large, rectangular, gabled structures, providing living and storage space for the extended household, and often built on platforms set on posts.

Household Animals

The animals domesticated in Southeast Asia—dog, pig, fowl, duck, and goose—are all animals of the household, in contrast

[28]

to the herd animals originating in Southwest Asia. As with the plants, the domestication may be attributed to the care and arts of the women who managed the household.

The dog is generally given place as the oldest domesticated animal, the eldest companion of man. There is no basis, however, for the story that as camp follower of hunters, he gradually joined the camp and became their hunting companion. This attractive myth is a projection into the past from modern European romantic views. Hahn long ago pointed out that hunting dogs are late specializations among certain peoples of advanced culture. Really primitive peoples do not hunt with dogs, though these may trot along with a hunting party. The great hunters of the Upper Paleolithic had no dogs. It has been noted that these appear archeologically first with Mesolithic folk, who were not much engaged in hunting, at least not on the land.

The Swiss zoologist Studer began a series of studies in the comparative anatomy of the dog and its relatives, which have been extended by others, especially in later years by Dahr of Sweden.[8] These make a strong case for the monophyletic origin of the dog. The conclusion is that the dog, in several ways less specialized than the wolves, cannot be derived from the latter, as on grounds of comparative anatomy man cannot be derived from the apes. Objections were raised to the conclusions of Studer since he postulated an unknown ancestor. Since then, however, remains of a wild dog have been described from the Early or Middle Pleistocene Chou-k'ou-tien caves near Peking, also of a recently extinct wild dog of the Tengger Mountains in Java. The feral pariah dogs and the Australian dingo are accepted as approximate models of the primitive dog. Dahr has reduced the so-called archeologic species of European dogs to breeds selected as domestic variants from a single ancestry, and considers that much later occasional wolf blood was introduced by Arctic hunters, as by Samoyed and Eskimo. The dog is considered therefore as originating from a wild dog, native to Southeastern Asia, living in forested monsoon lands, perhaps resembling the fox in food and social habits.

When Europeans set out to discover the seas of the world, they found the tropical villages of both Indies overrun with pets. Sailors returned, bearing monkeys, parrots, guinea pigs; soon there were pet shops and zoos to entertain the homefolks. Raising and training pets is still characteristic of both Indies. As I know it, the animals are always taken as young as possible. Men bring in fledglings from their nest, infant mammals are taken from the den or saved on killing the mother. I have had guides size up a young captive and then hit it over the head as too old to tame. Wildness develops rapidly in the young; only the helpless infants, wholly dependent on foster parent, form the strong attachment to the household in which they are raised. The feeding and training of the young captives is by women. The animals share roof and food of the family, are playmates of the children, and become part of the household. A comfortable surplus of food and permanent dwellings is presupposed, for the purpose is not economic at all. This is an important cultural bent, giving varied esthetic satisfaction; it merits study as to cultural context.

Infant mammals require milk. Until there were domestic mammals, the only nurse-mother available was woman. There are still tribes in tropical America and in Southeast Asia among whom women suckle pups, pigs, kids. By such means, the dog was actually adopted into the human family and into a specific family, within which the children were his kin. Under these circumstances, the dog may acquire a personal name and on death be mourned as any other member of the family. Somewhere, at some time, these ties became so strong as to result in domestication and the propagation of a stock that lost connection with the wild kin. It seems also that a good while ago the wild dog had become rare and this may have helped the absorption of the tame dog into human communities. In Southeastern Asia, the simpler peoples hold the dog in familiar and reputable status. It is here that the myths of a dog as tribal ancestor are most commonly found.[9] Even among the Chinese there is an elaborate legend of the marriage of an ever-faithful dog to a princess, with noble issue. Our western myths of Beauty and the Beast may have some similar origin.

In the Old Planting culture the dog, as a prized and respected creature, came to be an object of sacrifice, and of ceremonial consumption by the participants. As familial and religious connotations became blurred, the dog became a food item, especially at feasts. Because the dog held a position of high respect in this culture, it readily became an object of antipathy in neighbor cultures of other ceremonial and religious orientations. These latter rejected the animal as despised and unclean. It was, however, early disseminated into far parts of the world, farther it seems than any other parts of the culture from which it stemmed. In being handed on to peoples of other habits, the dog lost its status as member of the family circle, but became an utility animal, as watchdog, for hunting, for draft, for wool.

The wild pig of the Southeast Asiatic mainland, *Sus vittatus*, is unquestioned as ancestor of the domestic pig of that part of the world. The wild form is replaced by *Sus cristatus*, which has not been domesticated, in the formerly continental islands of Sumatra, Java, and Borneo. The *vittatus* species lives in jungle forests, likes to root in the village plantings, and does not avoid human settlements as does the European wild boar. The domestic pig too has become a member of the household and its domestication may have been by the same route as that of the dog. The spread of Hinduism and Islam has pretty well wiped out ceremonial uses, which persist, however, elsewhere.

Our domestic fowl stem from the jungle fowl of the less wet margins of the Bay of Bengal. The wild fowl weigh only around two pounds, lay settings of four to seven eggs, are shy, elusive, and keep away from settled areas. No economic motive is involved in their domestication: their egg laying and meat producing qualities were developed elsewhere and at later times. In Malaysia and India, their traditional use is for cock-fighting and this has resulted in selection for big bodies and broad breasts. Another ceremonial selection is shown by black color, including black skins and black bones, blackness still having magic and medicinal values. Our poultry fanciers maintain this originally ceremonial breed of Silkies, genetically weird, economically almost useless, but spread of old through eastern Asia.

All domestic ducks, except the New World Muscovy, are bred from the wild mallard. Little is known of their history but their diversity and importance in China, and in part also in India, are suggestive of antiquity.

Dispersal of Domestic Plants and Animals into the Pacific

The ancient complex of plants and household animals was dispersed far and early in all directions except northward, where cold blocked the way. The islands of the Pacific, as they were colonized by man, were stocked by introductions from the Asiatic mainland, ultimately as far as Hawaii and Easter Island. Be the cultures Melanesian, Polynesian, or Micronesian, the domesticates rarely are of island origin, but came from the Southeast Asiatic planting hearth. A number of plants, lost or largely lost to cultivation to the west, have been kept or have survived ferally in some of the islands, such as the primitive seed-bearing bananas, uncertainly named *Musa fehi,* pandans, certain inferior yams, and lesser aroids. That a planting culture got into the island world at a fairly remote time is suggested by diversification of races of some cultigens, as of the common breadfruit.

It is curious that the pig was not taken to New Zealand, while it got to other far extremities of Oceania. East of the Wallace line, all the pigs appear to be of *vittatus stock,* though the wild pigs of the island west of that line are of *cristatus* stock. The so-called wild pigs of Timor and New Guinea therefore are considered to be only feral. Beyond the limits of Islam, the pig is of major importance to man, as much so ceremonially as for food. That the dog reached Australia may possibly be due to a slight penetration of higher culture; the failure of sedentary folk to establish themselves in Australia whereas they found and occupied the smallest atolls in the wide ocean remains unexplained and cannot be ascribed to physical barriers.

Into China and Japan

South Chinese agriculture and that of Japan are advanced developments stemming from the original hearth to the south. Rice, bamboos, bananas, taro, persimmons, and yams, brought originally from India or Indochina, were greatly remade and diversified by man in East Asia before we can speak of either Chinese or Japanese peoples. Rice, for example, contrary to Chinese classical lore, is known from Neolithic settlements of North China. Planting methods were elaborated into the most sophisticated garden culture of the world. Warm climate plants were selected for shorter seasons and cold resistance and new domesticates were added from northern natives. Among those native plants vegetatively selected were the sedge *Eleo-*

charis tuberosa, the yam *Dioscorea batatas, Sagittaria,* and some of the citrus fruits. In the numerous Neolithic villages of the loess lands, large quantities of pig bones have been recovered.[10] The planting culture, spreading from the south, set the dominant pattern northward beyond the Yangtze and across southern Japan; of the household animals the pig and dog, at least, were carried well to the north.

Into Africa

In tropical Africa, agriculture is by planting, usually by women using either hoe or planting stick. The general configuration of life is remarkably similar to Southeast Asia, and the basic items are introduced from the East. The statement applies only to the forest people, not to those of the Sudan, nor to most of East Africa. The forest negroes have no great variety of cultivated plants. The great staple before the coming of European ships was plantains and bananas. A section of the genus *Musa* is native to Africa, but it does not enter into the parentage of the cultivated bananas and plantains, which are derived from India and possibly beyond and probably were brought around the northern margin of the Indian Ocean. Taro was similarly and also anciently introduced. The greater yam *(Dioscorea alata)* may have come late out of India, carried perhaps by Malays or Arabs. The wide presence of *Dioscorea bulbifera,* with cultivated races differing in Africa from those of the East, and of *Tacca pinnatifida* (called both Fiji and African arrowroot) need further examination. So may that of the tuberous *Coleus,* which Vavilov assigns to Southeast Asia, but which is more probably African. Scientifically, tropical Africa is still the Dark Continent. Two cultured yams are certainly of African origin, the white and yellow Guinea yams *(Dioscorea rotundata* and *cayenensis,* the latter misnamed as from the New World). Only a subordinate center of vegetative domestication can be credited to forest Africa, centering somewhere behind the Guinea Coast.

Of domestic animals, the dog and fowl have been widely distributed in Africa and what little is known of their races suggests ancient introduction. Both were found at the first white contacts with the pygmies and the Niam-Niam. There are some curious bits of information that may have bearing on the antiquity of African-Indian contacts. Strange negro fowl of black feathers, meat, and bones were described from Mozambique in 1635,[11] and there are hints of black fowl in negro ceremonies that need inquiry, as to breed as well as ritual. The pig has been reported only from the borders of Ethiopia, especially from the ancient land of Sennar between the Atbara and the White Nile, where there are surviving pre-Hamitic peoples and cultures. Some of these raise pigs and here there are also wild pigs, which, however, are only a feral form of the Southeast Asiatic *Sus vittatus*. The inference is that the pig was introduced from the East into eastern Africa, perhaps over the same route by which bananas, taro, and chickens were brought, but that it disappeared with the spread of Hamitic dominance or was lost in Abyssinia by the Semitic conquest. The Abyssinian Christian Church, it may be noted, bans the eating of pork. Europeans have found pigs difficult to keep in equatorial Africa because of tsetse-carried trypanosomes. The natives of West Africa have a partly domesticated bush pig of different genus *(Potamochoerus)*, from Guinea down to Angola. It is possible, therefore, that the Asiatic household pig met a barrier in the African forest and that a partial substitution has been made by a similar native animal.

Tropical Africa did not get its planting culture out of India by way of the Fertile Crescent. The bananas, for instance, could not take the northern route. The passage westward can hardly have been in any other manner than by skirting the Indian Ocean. Along it there was no winter cold and the arid stretches were broken at intervals by alluvial strips watered from highlands. The southern rim of Arabia, from the Straits of Hormuz to those of Bab el Mandeb, along the coasts of Oman, Hadhramaut, and Yemen, may be a great lost corridor of mankind. Coon has called attention to survivals of primitive human stocks here, small elf-like roundheads in the Yemen coast, in Hadhramaut Veddoid and negrito types as well as Mediterranean racial elements.[12] Schweinfurth found taro so naturalistically distributed in Yemen that he considered it a native plant. The door into Africa south of the Sahara was the Abyssinian highland and its foothills, inviting for primitive agriculture; the Sennar country was the last step on the route west into the tropical forest lands and the Sudan. This corridor between East Asia and Africa was used repeatedly in agricultural dispersals; it still awaits closer exploration. The carriage of plantains over this route presents no special difficulties. Although plantains produce fruit only with a good supply of moisture, they can withstand long dry seasons. Also, the root stocks can be thoroughly dried out and left exposed for months before replanting. In some places it is customary to expose the planting stock to long drying.

Into the Mediterranean

Parts of the Old Planter culture reached the Atlantic by way of the Mediterraean. The presence of the dog through the Mesolithic of Europe has been mentioned. The name of the Canary Islands is thought to refer to the dog-keeping and eating habits of the natives. Pig remains are common in early archeologic sites of the Near East and westward, as in Egypt at

Faiyum and Merimde, in Palestine at Gezer. Menghin,[13] in fact, has set up a swine-breeder culture at the threshold of the Neolithic, wide spread across southern Asia and southern Europe. He maps it on the basis of association of pig bones with certain artifacts, in particular with a sausage-shaped, chisel-edge celt or ax of greenstone. Domestic pig remains have been described from the first sedentary horizon at Anau and from the Lake-Dweller villages of the Alpine forest lands. In both cases, these have been determined as turbary pig, a form of the Southeast Asiatic *Sus vittatus*. Modern swine breeds in con-servative peasant communities of the Grisons in the Alps and in Transcaucasia are assigned to the same stock. The wild pig of Sardinia has been placed as a *vittatus* form and hence would be of human introduction.[14] Professor Gordon Ferris of Stanford tells me that the lice of our domestic pigs are not those of the European wild boar but of the *Sus vittatus*. All of which seems to add up to the conclusion that the domestic pig was passed on from India across the Mediterranean to western Europe, that such is the basic stock of our common swine, with subsequent incrossing of some boar blood. I know of no evidence of in-dependent pig domestication in Europe or in western Asia.

There are numerous indications that the pig belongs in the substrata of Mediterranean culture history. The Egyptian god of evil, Set, was identified with the pig, but he also was con-sidered eldest of the gods and suffered the degradation that happens to elder gods when later divinities gain adherence. Where vestiges of pre-Indo-European culture remain in the Mediterranean, the pig is likely to have a place of prestige. The Arcadians, ancient mountaineers of the Peloponnesus and in part pre-Dorian, were known as swineherds and acorn eaters. The greatest and oldest of the Greek mysteries, the Eleusinian, used the pig alone as cult animal. The place of the ritual oc-

[37]

cupied a pre-Greek cult site of high antiquity. Sir James Frazer in "The Golden Bough" shows the close association of Demeter-Persephone with the pig, suggesting that she may have taken the form of the animal, and that Demeter is a Greek version of the more ancient Great Mother. When Xenophon celebrated the approaching return to his homeland, he made burnt offering of swine, according to the custom of his country, which was Athens. Among the Romans, pork (*porcina* or *suilla*) was the preferred flesh, and the customary main dish at feasts. It was a common sacrifice, especially to the household gods, the lares, the familiar spirits that were older than the high gods. The ancient Iberians, pre-Indo-Europeans, were swineherds and esteemers of pork, as their partial descendants, the Spanish and Portuguese, still are. Far out on the last island of the Canaries, Ferro, lived the most primitive of the diverse natives of the Islands. They held in veneration the pig, according to one of the earliest accounts, "conscious that a demon appeared to them in such form."[15] These are samples of evidence of a pre-Indo-European, pre-Semitic pig culture and pig cult, which persisted in the West in spite of the coming of later gods and still later of Christianity, but which the spread of Semitic and Hamitic ways wiped out in the Near East and Africa.

Finally, across the Mediterranean, increasing in strength westward, the privileged position of woman is to be noted. The mother, and especially the grandmother, has authority over the family throughout Hispanic and Portuguese areas. The Basques are not only matrilineal, they have pretty much a matriarchal society, and the Basques are the clearest survivors of folk who came before the children of Shem, Ham, and Japhet spread their ways over the ancient world.

The plants of the Farther East either did not pass westward as did other elements of the Old Planter life, or they were dropped in favor of seed plants. The chufa, *Cyperus esculentus*, which is of old culture in the Iberian Peninsula, may be an exception. However, the Mediterranean agriculture relies on vegetative reproduction and selection in its own manner, and these ways are ancient. The two principal areas of horticultural skills are southern China and the old Mediterranean, with similarities in techniques, and both may well owe their original stimulus to ideas out of India. Among the oldest cultigens of the Mediterranean are the date palm, the olive, and the fig, all of them reproduced by cutting. The date palm either stems from a lost ancestor in the Near East or from the wild *Phoenix sylvestris* of western India. The olive and fig are first known from the eastern end of the Mediterranean and may have originated there (or in southern Arabia?). The alteration from wild ancestor into the cultured form in each of the three is great and would seem to require a formidable length of time. The immemorial manner of reproducing these plants rests on pretty refined horticultural practices of no casual origin. Yet, in so far as known, they are part of the oldest Mediterranean agriculture. The grape, out of mountain valleys of the Caucasus-Turkish-Iranian border lands, is also grown by cuttings; but it is thought to be later, principally because wine in Greece is younger than other alcoholic drinks. The difficult and tedious procedure of creating and reproducing the olive tree and of making olive oil is more readily derived from the disciplined planting arts first fashioned in India than from any other source. Also, only in that one corner of the Mediterranean facing the ancient East do we find the origin of cultigens according to the eastern model.

III

The Planters of the New World

Again, a Tropical Hearth

The lower latitudes of the New World hold an agricultural complex that resembles closely the one across the Pacific and may be the source out of which the farming ways of the New World were fashioned. It is a planting culture, especially well developed all about the Caribbean both as to mainland and islands, and it dominates most of South America. Even now, a line drawn through the Florida Straits into the Gulf of Honduras and then winding southward through Central America to the Pacific Coast in Costa Rica (Pl. II) approximates a separation between a northern and southern pattern of aboriginal farming. Between West Indies and United States mainland the separation is sharp, in Central America transitional. The Antillean farmers at the coming of the Europeans were Arawak and Carib, who had brought their ways from the southern *tierra firme* of the Caribbean. In Central America, the Caribbean side was occupied by natives of Chibchan affinities, living in the manner of their kinsmen in Colombia. The native stocks may long since have disappeared or have become blended into mestizo populations, but the plants and animals that are grown today and the habits of rural life still carry many qualities of ancient ways and days. This tropical culture is based strongly on the idea of vegetative reproduction.

Its origins are to be sought not in tropical rain forests, but in areas of alternate rainy and dry seasons. The seasonal rhythm about much of the Caribbean is not very different from that of the monsoon lands of Southeast Asia. In particular, to the south of the Caribbean Sea lie lands of very diverse climates, ranging from near deserts on the shores of Venezuela to the rain forests of the Andean montaña, both on the Pacific and in the interior, and to the Alpine páramos of the higher mountain chains. Between these extremes lie numerous intermediate climatic areas attractive to agriculture. The splitting of the Andes into a number of sierras and basins abutting against the Caribbean Sea brings rain shadow conditions to one position, rain increase to another. Ranges of sedimentary rock, of crystalline and metamorphic rocks, volcanoes of ash, cinder, and lava flows have resulted in extreme range of soils. To this high diversity of climate, terrain, and soils is joined a most varied flora expressed in patterns of distribution that led Humboldt to one of the earliest formulations of biogeography. Here the life forms that originated in the southern continent meet the immigrants from the north which moved down through the Central American land bridge and also others of Middle American origin. We know little of degrees of kinship between wild and cultivated forms for the New World, but the genera to which the vegetative cultigens belong are clustered about the Caribbean as nowhere else.

Northwestern South America is also at the human crossroads of the New World, both by land and sea. It has many waterways of streams and along sheltered coasts, with a lot of aquatic and riparian life useful to man, both animal and plant. It has many sheltered basins of fertile land, within which people could live well and increase and shape their own cultures with the proper balance of self-containedness and outside contact. Environmentally this was the land of greatest invitation for

[41]

riparian folk to become sedentary and to begin the experiments of domestication, the likeliest spot in the New World for agricultural origins.

Archeologically the area is still mainly unexplored. We know that metallurgy used most advanced techniques here, that a strange high civilization both of mountain and lowland had passed its peak before the coming of the white man, in particular in Colombia. It may not be accidental that the two greater historical areas of native high culture, the Peruvian and the Mexican-Guatemalan, lie near the opposite margins of the Caribbean *tierra firme*.

Ethnic traits have many resemblances to Indonesia. The natives were admirable boatmen and made dug-out canoes and pirogues of various and excellent designs. They were skilled net fishermen and used barbasco cunningly. Some of them were adept at preparing arrow and dart poisons that caused sensible losses to the Spaniards. They colored food and painted themselves with the fruit of the Bixa, whence, perhaps, the origin of the name red Indians. They made fermented drinks by chewing and used masticatories. The Spaniards found natives living in multifamily rectangular houses, many of them built on platforms set on posts (whence the name Venezuela) and not restricted to flood plains. Villages were surrounded by *palenques,* stockades through which the invaders had to hew their entry. The name cannibal is derived from the name Carib, and the Spaniards wrote gruesome accounts of the eating of human flesh, especially in western Colombia. Cannibalism is one of the less attractive traits that accompanies cognate planting cultures, both in Southeast Asia and Africa.

And, although the Spaniards were not aware of it, this was the first acquaintance of Europeans with an undisturbed matrilineal society. From Española to Colombia they met ruling

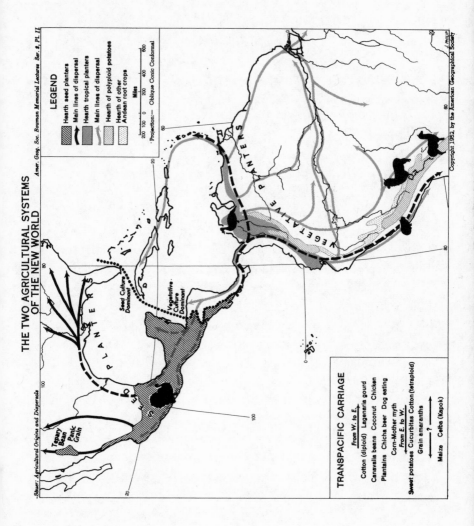

THE TWO AGRICULTURAL SYSTEMS OF THE NEW WORLD

Sauer: Agricultural Origins and Dispersals

Amer. Geog. Soc. Bowman Memorial Lectures Ser. 2, Pl. II

queens and princesses. The Spaniards were titillated and shocked by what they considered licentiousness and worse, the unfamiliar mores of a society in which the males did not make the rules. The pattern of behavior was so different from their own, that, as civilized people, they unhesitatingly condemned it and proceeded to break it down. Out of these confident ignorances they built the myth of the Amazons, in which there was some truth.

I like the combination of nature and culture in northwestern South America for locating here the first hearth of agriculture and so am disposed against seeking its origin or plural origins in higher latitudes. A single New World center is unproved (I once wrote in the opposite sense)[1] but it seems to me that there is a case for one basic hearth, and that case I shall try to present as an invitation to inquiry.

Brazil has often been designated as one of the centers of origin, in part, because a number of cultivated plants and their wild relatives were first described from southern Brazil and the La Plata Basin by nineteenth-century European naturalists. In land forms, soils, and climates, Brazil, like the eastern United States, is designed in large patterns, with gradual transitions, and hence it is a land of reduced floristic diversity as compared to the Caribbean lands. Culturally, it lies at the farther end of the New World. It is mainly a reservoir of primitive populations pressed into a dead end by more advanced cultures or untouched by innovations arrived at elsewhere. Numerous agriculturally attractive areas were inhabited by folk of simple collecting and hunting habits. The principal agriculturists belong to the Tupi-Guaraní family and are late arrivals in the south. Their earlier home appears to have been about the lower Amazon where they had been in contact especially with the Carib peoples; the culture they brought with them is hardly more than Caribbean. East of the Andes, Arawak tribes carried northern ways and plants by far flung colonies to the interfluves of Amazon and La Plata. South of the Amazon archeologic finds of sedentary populations, at least to date, are very meager.

The peanut is usually credited to Brazil because of related wild forms. It was never more than a subordinate crop anywhere and being a protein food, would not be expected to be one of the first domesticates in a planting culture. There are two principal lines to cultivated peanuts,[2] the one aboriginally better known, distributed from the Peruvian coast north to Mexico and, in so far as I am aware, unknown to the east of the Andes. It is fairly old in Peruvian archeology. Until further studies are made, the identification of the home of the cultivated peanut is uncertain.

The pineapple is also commonly said to be of Brazilian origin. Again, we have a minor cultivated plant. So-called wild pineapples have been reported from Brazil (earliest) to Venezuela and Colombia. Like most of the terrestrial Bromeliads, the plant is xerophytic and has numerous suitable habitats about the Caribbean. It was here that the Spaniards found the fruit most cultivated and most selected, and it was from here that appreciation of this king of fruits, as described by Oviedo and other early reporters, was spread. Its place of origin also remains uncertain.

Agriculture on the desert west coast of South America and in the higher Andes is probably derivative from elsewhere because the environment demanded advanced skills such as irrigation. Tello thought of the hearth as in the Amazon basin, but this tropical forest land seems unsuited both as to plants and culture. The port of entry for Peruvian agriculture I should place to the north, with some secondary later domestication moving up from northwestern Argentina (Diaguita culture). The vegetative cultigens of Central America appear to be assignable to Colombia, and its annuals to the North. Agriculture seems to have been introduced into the West Indies by the spread of the Arawak from the South American mainland. And thus I come back to the northwestern part of the southern continent as combining more favorable factors than any other area.

Tropical Plants and Tillage

Here again, planting is done by setting out cuttings, usually in mounds or ridges of top soil thrown up by spade-like tools. Selection was by division and multiplication of attractively varying clones. In contrast to the Old World there are no wetland domesticated plants. All thrive best with good drainage. Where drainage was poor the cultivators built the mounds high to provide aeration.

All the important food plants are grown for starch and sugar. Vegetable proteins and fats were as much neglected as across the Pacific. First among the starch products was manioc (*Manihot utilissima*), or yuca as it is called through most of Spanish America, the name having been picked up from the Arawak of the West Indies. Wissler thought it so important that he named the tropical Indian economy from it. It is widely grown in tropical forest lands on well-drained sites, but its home is not in the rain forest. The starch which it stores in its tubers enables the plant to make a quick start when the rains begin, and to sustain long dry seasons. Its native climate is that of the savanna with a rainless season longer than the rainy one. The yuca is extraordinarily drought resistant and for that reason has been so successfully introduced into Africa between the forest and the desert. I have seen it flourishing in Peru in soil so dry that cotton and grapes, both drought tolerant, were wilting. The plant, incidentally, looks somewhat like the castor bean to which it is related; its woody stalks are important as fuel. Reproduction by cutting has been carried on for so long that it has lost almost completely the ability to set seed. There are very many races, largely unstudied; the wild parent is remote and uncertain. It is certainly an ancient cultigen, bred to rank in yield with the bananas of the Old World. I should guess an origin in the Venezuela savannas, a tropical climate with marked dry season.

The bitter, or poisonous varieties of yuca have been distributed in Atlantic drainage basins from Cuba to southern Brazil; they were unknown in Central America, most of Colombia, and in the Pacific Coast of South America. In the montaña at the eastern base of the Andes they are likely to be absent among the more archaic folk, and present among tribes that have moved up the Amazon from the east, especially those of Tupi and Carib affiliations. The manner of preparation follows a fairly standard pattern of grating, pressing, and washing to remove the hydrocyanic acid, followed by baking into the admirable and long-keeping flat bread, called *cazabi* (cassava). The sweet varieties appear to be grown wherever bitter manioc is, but their cultivation extends much farther, into extratropical latitudes and altitudes. Sweet manioc is mainly boiled or baked, without grating, and rarely is the staple food that the bitter forms commonly are.

The sweet potato (*Ipomoea batatas*) is perhaps next in importance and extent of distribution. Its natural habitat also is one of opposed rainy and dry seasons, but it would seem to belong to a land of less drought than the manioc. The plants commonly flower in low latitudes, but very rarely seed. The general mode of propagation is as with us. Along the Pacific the sweet potato was grown beyond the limits of yuca cultivation, both

[46]

north and south. In interior South America Arawakan peoples seem to have favored its cultivation. Selection developed both sweet and starchy races, the latter giving the larger yields and hence perhaps of greater aboriginal use. The rapid and catastrophic collapse of Indian populations about the Caribbean by the Spanish conquest resulted in the loss of numerous varieties. Oviedo noted in 1526 that by that time some of the best kinds that he had known no longer existed. The Spaniards were not at all interested in the starchy kinds, but continued the cultivation of sweet races.

The peach palm, or pejibae (*Bactris utilis,* syn. *Guilielma*) is widely distributed through the warm lands of Colombia, into lower Central America, and south through the Amazonian montaña. It is grown from root sprouts. In many cases the fruits have only vestigial seeds. I do not know that it has been found truly wild; the so-called wild stands are perhaps only persistent groves about former settlements. The fruits are boiled or baked and have a chestnut flavor; food yield is high.

The New World aroid that takes the place of the taro, *Xanthosoma* (*yautia* or *malanga*), belongs in the main to the Atlantic tropics. It is still important in Puerto Rico and Haiti and in the northeastern mainland of South America. The lone New World cultivated yam (*Dioscorea trifida*) also has an Atlantic localization, especially in the Guianas and the West Indies. In the Caribbean also are the excellent but low-yielding American arrowroots, *maranta* and *allouia* (*Maranta arundinacea* and *Calathea allouia*) relict cultigens that may have given way to plants of greater productivity.

The racacha (*Arracacia xanthorrhiza*), a parsnip-like plant of high starch content, is much grown at temperate altitudes in the tropics, mainly in Colombia and southward through Peru in the mild inter-Andean valleys. All of these plants are reproduced by some practice of cutting, appropriate to the particular habit; all have been selected over long periods for their yield of starch and sugar so that wild ancestors are lost or unknown.

The planters of the American tropics were about as sophisticated as those of monsoon Asia in the use of toxic substances. Curare is used in modern medicine. In northwestern South America the arborescent daturas, known in our gardens as angel's trumpets, furnished narcotic drinks for initiation ceremonies which, according to dosage, bring visions, frenzy, stupor, or coma. These shrubs perhaps are known only as cultivated forms. Coca chewing and cultivation were pretty general through the south side of the Caribbean as well as in the Peruvian Andes. Tobacco may have been used first as a ceremonial drink, next in chewing and snuff, and perhaps last, by smoking. The elder cultivated species is inferred to be *Nicotiana rustica,* which was grown from Chile to Quebec, and seems to have originated as a hybrid on the Peru–Ecuador border. The milder and to us more acceptable species, our commercial tobacco (*Nicotiana tabacum*), is also a hybrid of two wild species, formed apparently at the edge of the tropical forest in or near interior Bolivia. The tobaccos and cocas are grown from seed, but in carefully prepared seed beds, from which they are planted out into the fields. A similar transplanting practice has been noted before in Southeastern Asia. There are several cultivated barbascos out of different families. The most famous one, *Lonchocarpus nicou,* a commercial source of rotenone insecticide, has been so fashioned to dependence on man that until recently it was thought to be incapable of flowering.

Animal Food

The only native, truly domesticated animal is the Muscovy duck, which has nothing to do with Moscow or with musk. The name may have come from the Muisca Indians of central Colombia. It is a tropical tree-nesting bird that pretty well avoids human habitations. The domestic forms still extend from the Araucanian villages of Chile to the northern limits of high culture in lowland Mexico. They were known to the Spaniards as *patos caseros*, house ducks, which they still are, their swimming and flying habits almost lost.

The lands about the Caribbean were also the center of a peculiar dog raising, a special breed of low slung dog being kept, often in pens, and fattened on plant food. The Spaniards, pressed a bit by hunger, found them delicious; the eating dog was one of the first casualties of the white conquest. In western Colombia there was semi-domestication of the pig-like collared peccary, which ranges from Texas to the Argentine, suggesting a parallel to the bush pig in western Africa.

In addition to fish, the tropical planters had available to them a remarkable wealth of aquatic and waterside animals— turtles, manati, water fowl, tapir, and the many hystricomorph rodents peculiar to this part of the world. The last are creatures of delicate flesh, ranging from the hundred and fifty pound capybara and the large pacas, to the little hutias and cavies. Some of these are now on the point of extinction, some became extinct before the coming of the white man, apparently due to overhunting.[3] The abundance and diversity of easily secured animal food and the absence of ceremonial motives for domestication may be a sufficient answer for the failure to domesticate more animals.

Planting in Non-Tropical Lands

Northward, vegetative planting was not carried far. It did not even reach the Tropic of Cancer despite the fact that the plants could have been grown far beyond. Southward it was spread to the farthest limits of agriculture, in the island of

Chiloé where the antarcticward limit of agriculture still rests. I like the idea that the highlanders learned the planting arts from the tropical lowlanders and that little by little, partly by selection, partly by substitution of other plants, the skills were spread from north to south into lands of cold, longer days and shorter summers.

Some of the tropical tubers, sweet potato and racacha in particular, do well in temperate altitudes, to six thousand feet or more. My postulated tropical planters, therefore, should have had no difficulty in settling valleys that reached well up into the Andes. For the next stage in the farming colonization of the Andes, that of the cool temperate zone, new crops had to be found. Among root crops, certain potatoes appear attractive possibilities to bridge the gap between *tierra templada* and *tierra fria*. A number of the simpler (diploid) cultivated species of potatoes which genetically are considered as early in the history of the elaboration of the cultivated potato complex, belong into these intermediate and mild climatic levels. Three of these have been identified for Colombia and Ecuador, and others from Peru and Bolivia, some of these latter out of intermediate, some out of high elevations. Of special interest is the papa amarilla, *Solanum goniocalyx,* still widely grown for its excellent quality and taste, planted in temperate levels.

In the first farming settlement of the cold country I should place emphasis on the second-rate tuber crops — oca, ulluco, and añu. The first is a cultigen *Oxalis,* the second of the *Basella* family of which we have the Madeira or mignonette vine in our gardens, and the last is what is popularly called a nasturtium (*Tropaeolum*). They are inferior in food value and in yield to potatoes, but are maintained in cultivation by highland Indians from Colombia to Peru and are grown in the same fields as potatoes. There are numerous races of each, and all three are man-made species, remote from any wild kin. It is difficult to believe that people who had passably satisfactory potatoes to hand would have given attention to transforming such wild plants into root crops which provided nothing that was not better provided by potatoes. On the other hand, if the minor tubers were developed first, they might retain a place in Indian cooking because of traditional dishes and old taste preferences. Wherever there are highland Indian communities these tubers still are much used; white people do not care for them.

The tubers of oca and añu are quite acrid and are commonly soaked before cooking. They are further improved if they are frozen, thawed, and washed repeatedly. The dried tubers thus prepared are called chuñu; they can be stored indefinitely and are easily transported. Today, chuñu processing is applied mostly to potatoes and the dry tubers are a major item of trade between the people living within the frost zone and those below. The process was perhaps first invented for the bitter tubers to make them more palatable and preserve them and later extended to the potatoes of the cold lands.

The history of the potato is better known than that of most plants, thanks in particular to the Russian and English potato expeditions into Latin America. The Russian group began the investigations, the English, under J. G. Hawkes of Cambridge, carried it forward, assembling impressive evidence of genetic connections, especially with the wild potato, and revising strongly the Russian interpretations.[4] Out of the genetically simpler (diploid) forms more vigorous, better-yielding polyploid forms have been made, especially the great tetraploid species complex of the high Andes of Peru and Bolivia, but also of Colombia, usually called *Solanum andigenum*. These and other high-yielding hybrids mainly enabled the denser agricultural settlement of the cold lands to altitudes above those of root crops elsewhere in the world. In time, *andigenum* potatoes were carried south to Chilean extratropical lowlands. This involved, with each move southward, selection for maturing under longer days. Chilean races, markedly of long-day habit, chiefly made possible the introduction of the potato into successful cultivation in northern Europe and thereby the agricultural revolution of the past centuries. It is to Hawkes that we owe the knowledge of the Andean derivation of the Chilean potatoes; he has finally disposed of the thesis that Chile was an independent center based on local wild forms.

Animal Domesticates

The Andean cultures domesticated llama, alpaca, and guinea pig. Of these, the guinea pig is perhaps the oldest. Professor Castle has made a good case for its domestication in the area of Arequipa, which lies close to the southern limit of the genus.[5] Such domestication close to the margin of natural range, where the animal was not abundant, has been noted for other animals. Genetic selection of the guinea pig has been especially for fecundity, size, and color patterns. The alteration from the wild form is great and indicates considerable age. The animal spends its life within the house, fed entirely by man. It has both ceremonial significance and food value. Mummified remains are common in desert burying grounds in north Chile. Professor Stirton informs me that the bones are abundant in archeologic sites around the savanna of Bogota. The guinea pig appears to have been well spread around the Caribbean. Early Spanish reports seem to refer to this household animal in the Antilles and Yucatan; and the English name is thought to be a corruption of Guiana.

The older center of llama breeding seems to have lain in the border country of Peru and the northwestern Argentine; for the alpaca, in the high mountains of the Peru-Bolivian border. All three of these animals, therefore, may have been domesticated within the territory that Richard Latcham ascribes to the ancient Atacameño people.[6]

Food Balance in the Andes

The peoples of the central Andes impress me as not having had a balanced diet. It certainly was, and in part is, distressingly low in proteins and particularly in fats. The Spanish improved the diet by introducing *habas* (*Vicia faba*) and field peas. The one native legume of the cold lands was the great seeded lupine *tarhui* (*Lupinus mutabilis*), an Andean cultigen, still fairly largely grown. It is pretty poor food and requires days of soaking before it can be eaten. Some of the potatoes have a fair protein content, such as the golden fleshed *S. goniocalyx*. Maize and quinoa also helped somewhat to make up protein deficiency. Maize, however, is less grown and much less efficiently used than in North America. The llama was no ordinary food; how largely the guinea pig was eaten is uncertain.

The highlands are miserably poor in fish, game, and fuel. Gilmore suggests extermination by hunting to explain the occurrence of several extinct animals found in archeological sites near Cuzco.[7] Guanaco and vicuña have disappeared from the larger part of their earlier range. These items indicate that man got seriously out of ecologic balance in highland Peru and Bolivia, that he overhunted animals as he overcut wood for fuel. The highlands once may not have been as bleak as they are now. The steady expansion of the Inca state may have been in part due to the need of more and better food for the protein- and fat-starved central highland.

[53]

Independent Invention or Diffusion

The general hypothesis that has been presented is that both tropical Asian and Andean planting cultures are environmentally divergent developments of one basic, dominant, and persistent way of growing and improving plants.

Not alone the vegetative manner of planting, but the overall configuration of customs and skills are much like monsoon Asia. And thus we come to the question as to common or independent origin. Did we have in the low latitudes of both hemispheres a generally similar solution of the opportunities present in the environment by parallel inventions? Or did the Planters of the New World in some degree derive their institutions and skills from the other side of the Pacific? Proof of the first thesis would show a remarkable "psychic unity of mankind" and power of environmental influences, similar environments giving rise to similar societies. This view can be established only by showing that there was no communication of planting peoples on the Asiatic side with the New World tropics; the opposite view requires evidence that there was such contact. The adherents of parallel invention have the advantage of representing what is considered the more respectable and conservative position. This rests not on evidence, but on authority: good scholars have frowned on the idea of such contacts. On the other hand, others, including geographers from Humboldt and Ratzel to Sapper, have thought that there was such diffusion of culture from the Old World to the New. The geographers, who by profession are students of the environment, seem to have least faith in the power of the environment to engender similar ideas in man. Also, perhaps we geographers find it easier to think of the earth as a continuous surface, for certain conveniences in map making represented as an eastern and western hemisphere.

That the Asiatic planting and fishing culture was expansive is shown by its spread across the islands of the Pacific and its penetration of tropical Africa, of the Mediterranean, and of western Europe. A diffusion about the northern margin of the Pacific should have presented no greater difficulties. Beyond Japan lie coasts and streams greatly inviting to skilled boatmen and fishermen. Here are the finest waters of the world for anadromous fish, such as salmon and sturgeon, the best crabbing grounds, and here were large numbers of sea-inhabiting mammals readily taken along shore, such as the Steller sea cow and the walrus. Inland seas and island chains provided sheltered harbors and facilitated water travel. Over most of the route growing timber or driftwood was available in abundance for boats and gear, for fuel and houses. It would seem strange that people who were adept boatmen and skilled fishermen and hunters on and by the water, should have held back from entering such coasts. They may well have continued to colonize northward from Japan, but have given up planting in the coasts of low summer warmth.

Numerous resemblances in customs between the Indians of our Northwest coast and peoples of Indonesia are familiar. In Kamchatka, the Alaskan Peninsula, Kodiak, and on the coast of British Columbia, there were matrilineal societies, living in multifamily houses with notions of property, prestige, and art forms which are about what might be left of Southeast Asiatic culture from which an adverse environment had eliminated certain possibilities, in particular agriculture.

As to archeology, we may have in the New World some equivalent of the European Mesolithic. Our earlier folk did not have the dog, bow, or arrow; when these were brought in, simple polished axes also appear, again mostly made of greenstone. This greenstone preference, which impressed Menghin

[55]

across the breadth of Eurasia, may not be coincidental for America.

The burden of denying passage to boat people having the skills mentioned would seem to me to rest on those who object to such diffusion into the New World. The passage may have been made at great leisure or it may have been made rapidly, by groups that leap-frogged from one fishing cove or stream mouth to another, to see what lay beyond. A few generations may have sufficed for a passage about the northern margin of the Pacific Ocean, during the spread of Mesolithic cultures.

It is reasonable in that case to consider that traditions of former planting practices might have survived, that a re-emergence of planting took place when the immigrants got to favorable latitudes, since the general cultural context remained pretty well intact. It is not beyond possibility that some plants were carried through, and this possibility needs to be studied. We have in North America a number of curiously distributed plants, commonly associated with man, of which we do not know the origin or whether they are identical with Old World forms. These include the sweet flag (*Acorus calamus*), the esculent *Cyperus, Trapa natans* (water chestnut), the Nelumbium lotus, and the *Sagittaria sagittifolia* of China and our Pacific Coast, known to the Columbia Basin Indians as *wapatoo*. Some of these plants are reproduced from underground parts, some have seeds of extreme viability; mostly their distributions are not such that animal or water transport seems likely.

Later there is varied and good evidence of transpacific carriage of plants in low latitudes, for which human agency alone appears competent. Again, there has been reluctance to get and to weigh the available evidence. The biological evidence is the most critical, since the same organism cannot be claimed to have originated repeatedly in distant parts of the world. Those opposed argue for post-Columbian introduction or accidental drift across the great Pacific by current and storm. Such explanations may strain the credible far more than do native boatmen who were able to venture into the open ocean. The post-Columbian explanations require extremely rapid handing on of the introduced thing over a very large area to accommodate the historically known presences.

Famous theses of this sort are: (1) the assumed carriage of the American sweet potato by Spanish vessels from Peru to the other side of the Pacific, and along with it the name "kumara," supposed to be Peruvian; (2) the presence of maize as an important Chinese crop of the second half of the sixteenth century as handed on in a few decades from Spain through the Mediterranean and southern Asia into China; (3) the bringing of bananas from Africa by Spaniards and Portuguese, as illustrated by the distribution of the supposedly European name *plátano* among the Indian tribes; and (4) the first introduction of the chicken into the New World by the Portuguese and Spaniards. Each of these constructions can be shown to be based on errors that invalidate them. I should like to present briefly the case of the chicken.

In 1922 Erland Nordenskiöld published a memoir on the spread of certain culture elements through South America.[8] One of the elements that he discussed was the domestic fowl. The known historical record begins with Magellan's party which secured supplies of fowls in 1519 from Indians on the coast of southern Brazil. Hence, so Nordenskiöld thinks, they were introduced by Cabral in the discovery of Brazil in 1500 or by someone else shortly thereafter. No document mentions anything of the sort, though the journals of Cabral's voyage are quite detailed. The Cabral landing took place a thousand miles to the north of the Magellan incident. In 1526 Cabot's men not only got hundreds of fowls in the coastal villages of South Brazil but sent for additional supplies to a distance of forty leagues inland. Later explorers of the interior from Paraguay to the Orinoco commonly found chickens being kept in Indian villages never before visited by whites. "Domestic fowls were evidently taken inland by Indian traders to far-off places long before these were explored by whites." Nordenskiöld elaborates this statement by lengthy and careful documentation. The name of the Inca Atahualpa is accepted by him as the Quechua word for domestic fowl; he traces the distribution of this name and other native names from the Araucanians to Amazonian tribes. "Not a single tribe living in an area bordering on the old territory of the Inca Empire calls the fowl *gallina* or *gallo* or uses any name traceable to Spanish." Doggedly Nordenskiöld worked out an enormous distribution of the fowl through remotest agricultural South America before Spanish contact, documenting it with the distribution of native names, ceremonial uses of the fowl, and selection for white plumage, as a remarkable example of explosive rapidity of diffusion. He did not concern himself with the question as to how chickens could have multiplied so rapidly as to have been spread over hundreds of thousands of square miles in a very few years, nor about the probable rate of acceptance of a strange new animal, including ceremonial acceptance, into a wide range of native societies. That the chicken could have been brought only by white men was a premise that it never occurred to him to question.

Ten years ago I went on a field trip in Chile with a Chilean zoologist. We were served boiled blue and olive green eggs at an inn. I was surprised at seeing them and he was surprised that we had no eggs of such colors. I then learned that the

Indians, that is, Araucanians, like to raise a breed of chickens that lays such eggs and that white folks do not care for such fowl or their eggs. We saw them in Araucanian village after village, obviously cross-bred with ordinary races. My education in the blue- or green-egg fowl continued at the hands of Don Ricardo Latcham in Santiago who, I found, knew a lot about the question and had written in the same year as Nordenskiöld another study on the chicken in the New World.[9] Using much the same documentation, he had come up with the opposite conclusion, that the Indian chicken was of a quite different breed from any European ones, that it had been introduced long before European contacts, and that it survived as the Araucanian fowl. Don Ricardo seemed to me to have the best of the argument. Few people seem to know this study of his, nor has this fine scholar and gentleman ever had full recognition outside of his adopted country for the range and depth of his insight into native cultures. To him belongs the credit for discovering the pre-Columbian chicken of the New World.

On returning home, I found that the blue-egg chicken was a *cause célèbre* in poultry genetics. Professor Punnett of the animal genetics laboratory at Cambridge had established this color factor as a dominant gene.[10] It is unknown in the Old World. Such dominant mutations arise very rarely under domestication, being ordinarily primitive genes of remote origin. The Cambridge experiments were made from Chilean stock. An Englishman resident in Costa Rica supplied Punnett with a further note of "original" chickens laying green eggs; this was among mountain Indians of Costa Rica, a small outlier of Chibchan culture surviving in mountain fastnesses. Thus, from the southernmost extremity of the New World vegetative planters to their northern limit there existed and in part still exists a greatly aberrant form of chicken, the like of which is unknown elsewhere. The Europeans could not have brought it, for they did not have it. Its economic qualities are inferior to European breeds and it survives vestigially as a marker of vanishing Indian cultures. Hybrid origin (which Latcham surmised) appears impossible for the New World has no nearly related fowl other than the turkey. A miraculous post-Spanish mutation can be ruled out; this is an Indian fowl, Indian cultures were in retreat and breaking down by Spanish conquest, and Chilean and Costa Rican Indians were not in contact with each other.

To the mystery of the chicken in the New World Dr. J. P. Harrison of our National Archives, adds a further item from the journal of T. A. Dornin, *U.S.S. Brandywine,* May 30, 1828, Paita, Peru: "The poultry here have black combs and black feathers, have also black meat, except a small white streak on their breasts—the bones are black, which is unfavorable in appearance only, for they are the sweetest and tenderest here. Prejudice is powerful, some of our mess would not eat them." This internal blackness has been noted for Asia and Africa as a quality of a ceremonial breed preserved in the ornamental Silkies. The source is apparently from Southeast Asia; an introduction by way of Europe is unlikely.

The transpacific carriage of cotton, the true gourd, sweet potato, and coconut appears proven, I should say, even for the coconut as due to the deliberate action of man. The case for the plantains, some eating bananas excepted, first proposed by Humboldt and supported by Sapper, is equally good, but has not been presented. There are several dozen plants, cultigens, intimately associated with man on both sides of the Pacific, that need critical investigation. Such plant remains in the pre-ceramic archeology of the coast of Peru show that times earlier than the Polynesian settlement of oceanic islands are involved.[11] Other culture elements that show up especially in Northwestern South America, such as chicha fermentation by chewing, masticatories with lime, the blow gun, perhaps the "edible dog," etc., may be inferred as introduced across the Pacific.

The principal aboriginal marine ports of entry may have been about the Peruvian–Ecuadorean border and their use lie as far back as the beginning of dynastic time in the Near East. Of significance, for instance, is the place of origin of the tetraploid cottons of the New World, originating out of Old World cottons and a Peruvian wild *Gossypium* (probably *G. raimondii*).[12] The crossings were in both directions; they did not introduce the planting system of the New World but they reinforced and enriched it with new items.

IV

Seed and Harvest

Seed Planting of Aboriginal North America

North of the Chibchan lands of Central America and the West Indies, the aboriginal mode of agriculture becomes quite different. Planting by cuttings is replaced by seed planting; selection takes place by sexual progeny, not by division. The northerners were seed farmers, making annual harvest and storage of matured seed, and selecting next year's seed stock from the pick of the harvest. With few exceptions the plants grown are annuals or became annuals by cultivation. I referred in the preceding lecture to this change in manner of plant reproduction as outlined fairly well as a hinge line, the contact of two great culture areas historically, differing also in other ways than by their agricultural practices (Pl. II). The Lenca of Honduras are of northern affinities, as are their neighbors the Mayan and Nahuan peoples, and as were also the vanished Otomangue and Subtiaba groups of the Pacific Coast.

Northward into Mexico, the dry seasons grow more marked and the highlands experience some winter cold, but environmental change is insufficient to explain the cultural change. In the coastal lowlands, root crops were grown well to the north of the hinge line, but remained subordinate to seed crops. In the Nahuan languages (of Mexico and south) the crop plants out of the south may have descriptive names indicating belated acquisitions, such as the name for manioc, *huauhcamote,* "the woody plant with tubers." The cultivation of

[62]

root crops stopped well short of the northern limits of Mexican high culture. No climatic barrier excluded the sweet potato from northern Mexico or the United States. By contrast, when it got into the hands of the Polynesians, races were bred that succeeded in the South Island of New Zealand, in latitude and climate similar to that of Vancouver. The folk north from Central America just were not strongly interested in the vegetative plants available to them from the south.

Nor did the north lack suitable wild plants to be grown and ameliorated by vegetative reproduction. There are wild *Solanums* in number in the highlands of Mexico and our Southwest that bear tasty and nourishing potatoes. Some of these by their genetic constitution and desirable qualities are of interest to our potato breeders. Wild *Solanum* species grow as volunteers in fields on the Central Mexican volcanoes. They are dug and eaten, occasionally are sold in the markets, but are not cultivated. In our Southwest, *Solanum fendleri,* the Navajo potato of sweet flavor and frost proof, is a wild food source that might have been an important addition to Indian agriculture, but the Pueblo farming tribes did nothing with it. In central and southern Mexico, various wild tubers, commonly called *camotes del cerro,* are dug and used as food, even sold by sidewalk venders in large cities, but remain uncultivated. The Indians of our eastern woodlands dug sweet tubers in quantity, such as the groundnut *Apios americana,* but they appear to have planted only seed crops; so too with the Jerusalem artichoke, which is not an artichoke and has nothing to do with Jerusalem. This tuberous sunflower is a persistent weed of cultivated ground and was common in Indian fields in Canada and the eastern United States, where it was a food item of some importance. Like the wild potatoes on the Mexican volcanoes, it multiplies well under disturbance by digging and this appears to have been the means of its increase and spread. Its actual selection in cultivation came at European hands.

The Maize-Beans-Squash Complex

The dominant plants of North American agriculture were maize, beans, and squashes or pumpkins. These formed a symbiotic complex, without an equal elsewhere. The corn plants grow tall and have first claim on sunlight and moisture. The beans climb up the corn stalks for their share of light; their roots support colonies of nitrogen-fixing bacteria. The squashes or pumpkins grow mainly prone on the ground and complete the ground cover. In lands of short growing season, all three may be planted together at the same time, the corn then being of early maturing kinds. In lands of long season, the corn was planted first, the other two later in the hills of corn. With few exceptions, all three were grown together. By long cultivation varieties of all were selected, able to grow to the farthest climatic limits of Indian agriculture. Civilized man has not extended the limits of any of them and has introduced only a few crops that succeed under more extreme climates. Maize, beans, and squash were grown on the lower St. Lawrence and by the Mandans on the upper Missouri. They are grown in *milpas* on the Mexican volcanoes to the highest patches of available soil. Forms were successfully selected for growing on the margins of the deserts of Sonora and Arizona where there is only an occasional summer thunderstorm. The Hopi, living in a land of little and late rain, of short summers and cold nights, depend on them and by them have maintained themselves and their fine and gentle culture, our civilization lacking the skills to match theirs for this harsh environment.

Maize is a species complex, the enormous diversity of which

is being uncovered by geneticists, mainly by study of Indian varieties. Only a small part of this genetic wealth is preserved in our commercial corns, which have been developed for rich soils and yield of grain, in part, as has been found lately, to the detriment of food value other than carbohydrates. Our main interest in corn is as feed for livestock; native attention has been given to it as a staple of human food. The corn on Mexican or Guatemalan hillsides that may seem a sorry plant to the visitor from the United States, is likely to be very properly suited to the native diet and the local soils and weather. The experiences of very many generations of corn growers are not to be set aside lightly by the simple and short-range interests of commerce. It is not accidental that a single native village may maintain more kinds of maize than the Corn Belt ever heard of, each having a special and proper place in the household and the field economy.

There are at least four quite distinct cultigen species of beans. One, *Phaseolus coccineus,* the scarlet runner bean, still is a perennial, used not only for its oil-rich beans but for its starchy, thickened root. Its cultivation extended at least from the Pueblo Indians of our Southwest to Ecuador and is greatest in the high country of southern Mexico, for it is mainly a cold country crop. The common kidney, navy, or frijol bean (*P. vulgaris*) has been most diversified and most widely spread; it is usually the dominant bean in the temperate areas, but there are important races to the limits of New World farming. The lima and sieva beans (*P. lunatus*) have their center of diversity in Central America, extend far south in South America, are approximately absent in Mexico, and reappear among the Pueblo and eastern-woodland Indians of the United States. Their distribution presents unsolved problems of dispersal.[1] The tepary (*P. acutifolius,* var.) is the Indian bean of Sonora and adjacent Arizona as well as the lower Colorado Valley; it is specialized beyond all others for least moisture and most heat requirements. The aboriginal farmers perfected beans suited to virtually all climates and soils, of high protein and oil content, and so superior to the pulses of the Old World that they soon became important additions to Old World gardens from western Europe to China and Japan.

Problems in the Distribution of Cucurbita

The genus of *Cucurbita* in its wild species is restricted to the New World. Wild variety is probably greatest in Mexico. Of the five cultigens, one, *C. ficifolia,* stands apart; in the appearance of plant and fruit it resembles a watermelon, and it is the only perennial cultigen in the genus. Its origin is assigned to the highlands of Mexico and Central America, where it is the only squash cultivated in the higher and colder fields. It is used a little as a green vegetable, somewhat for its seeds, and also for making a lightly fermented drink with the addition of sugar or honey. At present it is also grown as food for hogs, but otherwise is little thought of. In the Andean Highlands, it has very much greater importance in Indian food but has been thought to be a Spanish introduction into South America. No native name is known for it in South America, and one of the common names is a modification of the Mexican name, *tzilacayote.* Since this cucurbit is quite below the white man's notice, it is not apparent why Spaniards should have carried it into the southern continent. Lately it has been discovered in large quantity in the oldest archeologic levels of Peruvian coast agriculture, before pottery was made and before corn or true beans were grown there.[2] It is, therefore, the oldest cultivated squash known and it is archeologically known from a climate in which it is now absent. Its primitive qualities thus seem to mean, not that it is late and a marginal substitute where better squashes will not grow, but that it was early and was dropped from cultivation, except in cold areas, when better squashes were developed. Its historical position is reversed by these unexpected archeologic finds, and they reopen the question of the time of its appearance in the Old World. *C. ficifolia* was first described botanically from India where a different form, growing in a quite different climate, has long been known as the Malabar gourd. It is also known as the Siam gourd. A century ago some yaks from the borders of Tibet were shipped via Shanghai to France. Because it was thought that they needed accustomed food, a large quantity of this squash was brought down with them for the ocean voyage. Some were left over on arrival in France, the fruits having extraordinarily long-keeping qualities.[3] This plant of ancient American cultivation and of no economic use to the white man needs looking into as to its Asiatic forms and distribution. When such a study is made, the Asiatic forms of *C. pepo* and *moschata* which have perplexed botanists from Linné to Vavilov need also to be re-examined.

The other four cultivated squashes may form one cognate group, originally centered on the south half of Mexico. Our common field pumpkin, *C. pepo,* is dominant in the cool highlands of Mexico where it is a staple food. Diversity is low in Mexico and increases into the United States, especially east of the Mississippi, where it was carried as far as maize and the common bean. The great squash of the temperate lands of Mexico and Central America is *C. moschata,* which was carried about the Caribbean and to the coastal oases of Peru, where it met *C. maxima.* The purely South American *C. maxima,* grown from Chile across to southern Brazil, may have an ancestor in a wild gourd of the La Plata drainage, *C. andreana,* or *andreana* may be only "a weedy by-product or non-horticultural form of *C. maxima.*" However, since *andreana* "seems to be more closely allied to the perennial species, *C. ficifolia,*" the latter, introduced from North America long ago, may be involved in the ancestry of the South American squash complex.[4] *C. moschata* may also be involved. Whitaker and Bohn[5] have shown that it will cross with *pepo* and also with *maxima,* but that these latter two can be crossed only with difficulty. At present it looks as though *moschata* were the central and fundamental species, domesticated from some wild Mexican *Cucurbita,* all of which, as far as known, are perennial, with woody turnip-shaped roots. A *moschata* cross with another wild *Cucurbita* may have given rise to the pepos, near or beyond the United States border. The fifth species, ineptly named *C. mixta,* has been least studied. It is most easily recognized by a greatly swollen, corky peduncle, often bigger than a man's fist. It is now limited in distribution mainly to the hot lowlands of northwest Mexico and is the common squash of Sonora. Prehistorically it was grown on the southern Colorado Plateau, of brief, cool summers; it included a race that was used as water jugs by the cliff dwellers.

Wild *Cucurbita* and, even more so, those of the related North American genus *Apodanthera* are still collected and sold in Mexican markets for their seeds, edible on roasting. That the *Apodantheras* were not made into cultivated plants may be due simply to the fact that their range is mostly beyond the northern limits of the earlier agriculture. Here and there a cultivated form of thin-fleshed *moschata,* is still grown only for its seed. Throughout Mexico, squash seeds are carefully saved for food; indeed, to many Mexicans the seeds are quite as important as the flesh. The original domestication was for the seed. The wild kinds, in so far as I know them, are fleshless. Any mutation toward fleshiness was probably disadvantageous in natural reproduction. In the course of time cultivated variants were selected for their starchy and sugary flesh, and large forms developed. In many native and mestizo communities of Mexico and Central America, the large fruited races are about as important as corn or root crops as a source of carbohydrates; the seeds also are a principal source of protein and oil, hence in those countries the squashes are a principal staple food.

Multiple Use of Seed Plants

Everywhere the squashes have multiple and continuing uses and thereby illustrate an important characteristic of New World seed plants. The squashes have separate male and female flowers and this distinction has been well noted by the natives. Most of the male flowers are picked and used in stews, soups, and salads, enriching the diet with caretin. The young fruits are thinned from time to time to serve as green cooked vegetables; proper thinning secures maximum size for the fruits that are left to mature. The mature squashes are stored for consumption during the dry or winter season and may last until the next crop is in. Where a dry season is absent, they may be sliced and dried. The squash is likely to have, therefore, a year-round place of importance as carbohydrate food. The seeds are carefully taken out and dried. Roasted, they are either eaten out of hand or ground and mixed into meal or sauces. Hard-rinded forms may be scraped out and used as gourds for storage; the United States Indians also grew inedible gourd forms of *pepo,* used by ourselves in former days as darning eggs and now grown as ornamentals.

Other major New World seed plants are similarly used at various stages of their growth, as greens, for their inflorescence, for immature fruits, and finally when matured. This is true of corn, the beans, amaranths, and chenopods. They are alike vegetables and seed crops. Something may be taken out of the field at most times during the period of growth and thus they are distinguished from the Old World seed culture, in which the plants mainly are left untouched until the harvest. In large measure, harvesting is of single matured plants, not of the common maturity of a field. Also, there is no hurry about harvesting unless it is to save from damage by animal depredation. A lot of our native crops like corn and squash can await the convenience of the farmer. Harvest time has a less conspicuous position in the agricultural calendar of the New World than in the Old; harvest festivals are less important.

Planting Practice and Seed Selection

The native seed farmers of the New World still are in effect planters. Unless they have learned to plow, there is no overall preparation of a field, but selected spots are dug up, worked over, and heaped into mounds or hills. Each mound is planted with a number of things. The seeds are stuck into the ground, usually one by one; so many grains of corn according to the kind, so many beans, so many squash seeds, and perhaps some of something else. Selection of next year's seed stock is by individual plant. Individual ears of corn, entire seed heads of amaranth and chenopod are selected and hung up for the next season's planting.

By individual selection of seeds, the New World beans have acquired a large diversity of seed size, form, and color, which the mass-selected Old World *Phaseoli* lack. Both groups started with quite small seeds; but even our least teparies have been selected into seed sizes greater than those of any Oriental beans and many of the limas are giants. For ages our Americans have been playing around with size, color and shape of beans by sorting out the individuals that attract them; and they still do such hand sorting. The attention to individual plant qualities may well be linked to the planting of cuttings of attractive individuals.

Origin as Attractive Weeds

The ancestors of most New World seed plants appear to have been attractive weeds. They were not tenacious intruders that the cultivator had difficulty in getting rid of, nor are they such as grow on trodden ground. They were gentle, well-behaved weeds that liked the sunshine, loose earth, and plant food of the tilled spaces, and had no great root system. Such volunteers, usable by man, were first tolerated, then protected, and finally planted. The tomato is in part still in the stage of becoming a cultivated plant. In many places in Mexico and Central America the little cherry tomato is the common form; it is not planted, but protected. It, in turn, derives from wild, inutile tomatoes of northwestern South America.

I infer that other plants were grown before seed plants became the object of cultivation. Plantings of root crops provided room for self-sown plants. It appears that these volunteers which became cultigens are distributed especially around the farther margins of vegetative planting. Chile, at the southern limit of agriculture, has at least two native seed plants, the oil plant *Madia sativa* which is a tarweed, and *Bromus mango,* a weedy grass used as a minor cereal. In the northern periphery of the root crops a similar substitution on a much greater scale took place with amaranth, chenopod, squashes, and beans. It may be as simple as this: where climatic advantage shifted from the root plant to the seed plant, the attention of the cultivator shifted from the former to the latter. Instead of selecting root variants to meet the local situation, he began to select the attractive weeds.

[71]

Major New World Hearth of Seed Plants

I incline to the northwestern extremity of vegetative planting, that is, the Mexican–Central American border, as the hearth of the principal seed plants. In wild kindred, the squashes, beans, amaranths, chenopods, sunflowers, capsicums are best represented here. Their cultural diversity is also greatest here. Small-seeded and wild-colored races in particular are likely to be found in Mexico and northern Central America. The lima bean gets its name from Peru, but all the beans of Peru and most of those of South America are genetically recessive forms, of maximum seed size and of domestic colorations. The archeologic beans of Peru are scarcely distinguishable from present day commercial varieties. The earliest farmers there had no true beans; when these appeared, they were of highly-bred types. They were therefore brought in from elsewhere, long after domestic amelioration. Seed planting is distributed through most parts of South America. Seed plants are, however, usually subordinate to vegetative plants in the economy; their kitchen uses are fewer and simpler than in the North. Fewer kinds of squashes and beans are grown. Maize is considered by some specialists as of South American origin; yet there it is rarely the staple food, rather is it prized as a green vegetable, ears in the milk stage being much used, a low-efficiency use compared to the dominant Mexican use as *nixtamal*, wet ground hominy. In some South American areas aboriginal maize production was mainly for the making of chicha beer, again inferior to the Mexican malting. The argument of the origin of this mysterious monster continues among the specialists and we shall await its outcome. It seems to me too improbable a plant to belong to the start of the seed domestication complex. I prefer the view that it took place later and became substituted for the grain amaranths and chenopods, which from present evidence came out of the North.

The Turkey

The lone contribution of the American seed planters to animal domestication is the turkey. The wild form does not occur south of the Isthmus of Tehuantepec and the domestication took place in Oaxaca or some place nearby.[6] Other attractive birds, some gallinaceous, readily tamable and often kept tamed, were not domesticated. Among them are the handsome ocellated turkey of Central America, the curassows, and the whistling tree ducks, often kept as a sort of watch animal. The turkey of the Pueblo Indians I think was kept rather than domesticated.

Seeding Marginal to Planting in the Old World

In the Old World, at least three centers of seed domestication may be identified, all on the margins of the Old Planting lands. One lay in North China, including the loess lands, beyond the cold limits of the subtropical vegetative crops. A second began in western India ("India," throughout, is used in the traditional sense) and extended to the eastern Mediterranean, involving passage from summer rain to winter rain country. The third was in Ethiopia where the Abyssinian highlands adjoin the Sudan. In all three, vegetative reproduction was made difficult, annual seed growing facilitated by climate. The thesis that in climates marginal for vegetative planting, attractive volunteer seed plants became objects of use and of cultivation may also be applied to these three areas. In each, a cultivated assemblage took form that included starchy seeds, seeds rich in protein, and those yielding vegetable oils. These areas no longer depended on fish and other water or stream-side

[73]

animals, but acquired plants suited for balanced vegetarian diet. The Neolithic domestic pig continued to be important in North China, as it anciently was in the lands west from India and in the Ethiopian center. (The three centers are shown on Plate III.)

In each, the basic complex includes grasses cultivated for grain, legumes for protein and fat, and usually some additional oil and perhaps fiber plants. The plants that became the cultigens either were annuals to begin with, or were converted by selection into annuals. Much less so than in the New World were uses established for immature plants; a harvest season marked the high point of the year.

The basic grains were millets, a botanically meaningless but economically valid term. A millet is any small and many-seeded grass grown for its seed as human food. They were attractive for the multitude of seeds a plant produced, not for their size. Selection seems to have paid little attention to increasing seed size, but rather the size of the seed head. Grasses with many branched seed heads or panicles were sought after, such as the sorghums or those that set numerous seeds all about the spike, such as fox-tailed millet. The so-called great millets of travelers' accounts are mostly sorghums, the lesser millets may be of various grass tribes, but are in many cases some panic grass. In many countries of Asia and Europe a particular millet has a special odor of antiquity as traditional food, in folk lore, or as an early beer grain.

I do not consider the sites of early seed agriculture to have been grassy plains in the Old World any more than in the New. I accept the view of Vavilov that cultivation started in small valleys and their adjacent slopes, in mixed and varied vegetation. This is a rude departure from the cherished view that the earliest seed farmers avoided wooded and brushy land and

DOMESTICATION AND DISPERSAL OF SEED PLANTS AND HERD ANIMALS
IN SOUTHWEST ASIA AND NORTHEAST AFRICA

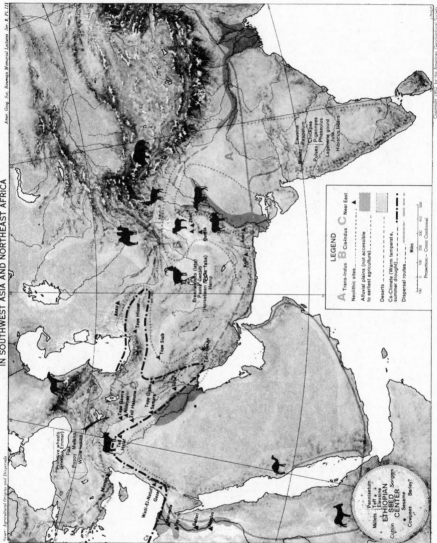

Sauer: Agricultural Origins and Dispersals

Amer. Geog. Soc. Bowman Memorial Lectures Ser. 2, Pl. III

LEGEND

A Trans-Indus B Cis-Indus C Near-East

▲ Neolithic sites

Alluvial plains (not accessible to earliest agriculture)

Deserts

Cs-Climate (Warm temperate, summer drought)

Dispersal routes

Miles
0 100 200 300 400 500

Projection:– Conic Conformal

Copyright 1952 by the American Geographical Society

ETHIOPIAN SEED CENTER
Pennisetum Sorghum
Millets Teff Eleusine
Cotton Sesame
Cowpeas Barley?

Eleusine
Millets Paspalum
Chickpea
Pulses: Pigeonpea
Phaseolus
Lagenaria gourd
Juba
Hibiscus fibers

settled in grasslands. As I said before, I inferred earliest settlement on loess because it was well drained, fertile and wooded and the soil was easy to dig (p. 21). The removal of tree trunks and brush did not become necessary until plowing demanded well-cleared areas, free from obstruction to the making of furrows.

During Neolithic time the surface was loosened by primitive spade or hoe, more often a pick than a transverse blade. Since small seeded things were grown, there was not the need of deep working that root crops required. The seed planters of the Old World seem not to have carried over the habit of hilling the ground which was continued in the New World. The small seeds needed to be only lightly covered; complete tillage of a field and broadcasting or drilling came probably with the later use of the plow. In the Sudan the ground is still, in places, loosened with a pick-like hoe, a hole dibbled with the big toe, a few seeds dropped and covered by a swipe of the foot, a good early model of seeding. Further cultivation was mainly by pulling weeds. Harvest required no special tools; the ripe seed heads were broken off or pulled, as is still done in parts of India and Africa.

North China

Bishop reported *Panicum miliaceum* from the Neolithic of North China. He says that "in the early writings this is the chief cereal mentioned, and it is the only one to possess a religious significance—itself a sign of great antiquity." [7] Vavilov and his associates assign to North China the origin of this ancient cultigen, a matter of considerable interest since it was also grown by the lake dwellers of the Alps. To China too, they confirm the origin of the foxtail millet (*Panicum italicum* or *Setaria italica*) which also was early in European cultivation, and either to China or Japan the barnyard millet (*Echinochloa* or *Panicum frumentaceum*). Thus the genetic evidence is that from this far source the panic millets were carried at an early time to India and the Mediterranean. They are ancient beer grains in Asia; as Bishop pointed out, fermentation was started by chewing, as with the vegetative planters to the south. This practice has a continuous Asiatic distribution and was diffused from a southern center.

North China produced the soy bean, a long-day plant which we are only now breeding to succeed in lower latitudes. This photoperiodism may have blocked its spread in the past; at any rate, it did not get carried as did most cultivated plants of high merit. Soya protein is equivalent to animal proteins for human food and said to be unequalled in this respect. It is also unequaled as a vegetable oil source. Two minor beans bridge the climatic gap between the great soya of the north and the beans originating in India. These are the adzuki (*Phaseolus angularis*) and the velvet bean (*Mucuna hassjoo*), the latter ameliorated from a genus marked by irritant and stinging pod hairs.

Ethiopia

At the other end of the Old Planting area a seed center took shape long ago in Ethiopia. Here, along the passageway by which taro and banana, hog and fowl were brought to Africa, a greatly different seed domestication had its home, from the temperate mountain valleys of Abyssinia to the hot Sudan and Saharan margins. It remained for Vavilov and his co-workers to discover in Ethiopia one of the world's greatest and oldest centers of domestic seed plants.

The home of the sorghums is Africa, the cultivated forms stemming from the general area of Ethiopia. The one exception is Johnson grass, now known to be a polyploid derivative weed and not ancestral to any of the cultivated sorghums. The great millet, the durras, and sweet sorghums were fashioned here, and from here stem the large number of secondary sorghum races of India, and the kaoliangs of North China. The pearl millet, or bajra of India *(Pennisetum spicatum)* is placed here, as are teff *(Eragrostis abyssinica)*, and, probably, the African millet or Indian ragi *(Eleusine coracana)*. Nowhere else in the world were so many or such valuable millets developed, a fact of major significance for the age of seed agriculture here.

Vavilov goes much further: "According to the number of its botanical varieties of wheat, Abyssinia occupies first place. In fact, botanical, physiological, and genetic studies indicate that the wheats of Abyssinia should actually be divided into separate botanical species. This is also the center of origin of cultivated barley. Nowhere else does there exist in nature such a diversity of forms and genes of barley." [8] I should interpret this to mean that barley, according to Vavilov, was originally domesticated here, and that certain local wild wheat grasses entered into the complex series that we call wheat, but that other areas to the north and east had an earlier role in the making of the wheats. Elisabeth Schiemann, in a recent publication, disagrees in a number of important conclusions with Vavilov. She assigns the origin of barley to eastern Asia (Tibetan-Chinese borderlands?); her new material suggests that this cereal may have been developed in the cold mountain borders either of China or India.[9]

To the pulses the area contributed the cow pea *(Vigna sinensis)*, the hyacinth bean *(Dolichos)*, and an anciently divergent lot of lentils (the Abyssinian forms are partially sterile with Asiatic ones). Sesame is originally a North African plant, and the gene center of the cultivated forms is here. The

[77]

list of Ethiopian contributions to the food plants of Old World agriculture is imposing.

Lately, a group of British cotton geneticists have overhauled thoroughly the previously badly confused picture of the genus *Gossypium* and related malvaceous plants.[10] Some of their findings have upset the earlier views of the New World cottons; another result, unnoticed by culture historians, upsets the Asiatic domestication of cotton. Only cultivated, man-made cottons they say are lintbearing. All wild species of *Gossypium* are lintless; any mutation toward lint is unsuited to survive in nature. The domestication of *Gossypium* seems to have commenced, therefore, before it filled its bolls with fiber and must have been for some other end, possibly for its oil-bearing seeds or fibrous stalks. The new view derives the cultivated Asiatic cottons not from an Asiatic wild species, but from the African arid-border *Gossypium anomalum,* thus opening a vista into a remote time when a Gossypium was first taken under the care of man in Africa for some unknown purpose, and later, presumably in Asia, was made into a seed fiber plant.

Archeology has never pointed a finger at Ethiopia as a cradle of civilization, but this and other biologic evidence does so, and very strongly.

West from India

West of the rainy monsoon lands of India rice and the root crops are replaced by annual seed crops, including protein and oil sources. Western India is not credited with many early cereal grasses, except for such minor ones as Koda millet (*Paspalum*), jungle rice (*Echinochloa colonum*), and Samai millet (*Panicum miliare*). It is a poor lot; something seems to be missing or lost. Some of the great west-of-India crops are African, such as the sorghums; wheat came from farther west.

[78]

Barley is certainly of ancient cultivation in India, and the Schiemann argument may place its origin nearby, probably to the northeast. Possibly these superior plants replaced earlier natives; that their Indian age is high is supported by their local diversification, as Vavilov pointed out. The rest of the list is better. Here are assigned four out of the five cultigen *Phaseolus* beans of the Old World, which moved also into China but not westward. Western India is the home of the chick-pea or garbanzo (*Cicer*), of old cultivation also in the Mediterranean. Here too is thought to be the first home of the widely wandered true gourd (*Lagenaria*), of the dish-cloth gourd (*Luffa*), the cucumber, eggplant, radish, lettuce, and hemp.

West of the Indus and north thereof, the rainfall still comes mainly in summer, but the season of rain is shorter and there is marked winter cold. Northwest India, Kashmir, Afghanistan, and eastern Persia are continental-climate extensions of the trans-Indus country. Additional important legumes were domesticated here: lentils, true peas, grass peas, and later this was the place of origin of the polyploid bread wheats.

Still farther west, beyond the deserts of central Persia, the lands of winter rainfall begin in the highlands of western Persia. This eastern end of Mediterranean climates is linked to cis- and trans-Indus lands in its crop plants. The legumes are almost wholly of more eastern origins, but, to the west, they appear in advanced, especially in larger-seeded, races.

The primitive wheats, alone among important crop plants, seem to have their roots in the eastern margins of the Mediterranean. The most primitive (diploid) cultivated wheat, einkorn (*Triticum monococcum*) is thought to stem from the highland borders of Asia Minor. Better wheat became available to Neolithic farmers in tetraploid cultigens, especially emmer (*T. dicoccum*), for which origin has been placed in Syria and

Palestine. (Schiemann again partially dissents, placing the home of emmer in the mountain borders of Anatolia, Transcaucasia, or western Persia.) It continued to be the great wheat of the Mediterranean through most of Roman time. The small-seeded so-called ancient bread wheats of the Near East are still unsolved, but McFadden has advanced an argument that these were actually a tetraploid species, similar to or identical with Persian wheat, and that bread wheat (*T. vulgare*), a hexaploid, came much later, developed in the Afghan-Indian border. At any rate, the Near East did have a leading part in the fashioning of wheat culture, but got most of the rest of its plants out of the East.[11]

The significance of wheat and also of barley in the early civilizations has perhaps been overestimated, possibly because they belong to our own system. That the Mediterranean lands and the Near East made more use of wheats than did others, is true. Why they did so is clear to me only in so far as these were winter crops. The millets began, and are mainly grown in lands of summer rain. Barley also is more largely spring than fall sown, though there are old races of winter barley. The winter-rain country of the Near East got from the Middle East such climatically adaptable crops as the chick pea, the field and garden peas, lentils, and Brassicas; but there may have been a climatic dilemma as to grains.

There were at the eastern end of the Mediterranean and farther east local wild *Triticums* and other grasses that cross to some extent with wheats, and some of these became improved at the hand of man. I do not think that these spindling plants of few seeds were very attractive, but they may have been the best available. Nor do I think that there were waving fields of wild wheats, waiting to be reaped by the sickle. Rather, the ancestral cereal grains would seem to have grown inter-mingled with a lot of different plants. Sickles, of sharp-edged stones set in wood, are an ancient tool of the Near East and, I think, have been correctly interpreted as a grass-cutting tool. They appear not only in the proto-Neolithic site at Tell Hassuna (Mesopotamia) but in the late Mesolithic Natufian.[12] I doubt, however, that they were used in the reaping of wild grass seeds. It is the nature of wild grasses, and especially of the wheat kindred, for the mature axis or rachis to be brittle and shatter, scattering its seeds to the ground. One of the principal changes by domestication has been the selection for non-shattering quality. Primitive harvesting of grass seeds is by seed beaters and baskets. A sickle, and especially a stone sickle would have lost the seed. The presence of the sickle is an argument for already domesticated grain.

The Pattern of Spread of Seed Agriculture in the Old World

It seems to me that the patterns of distribution of the seed annuals make some sense as to the manner of their dispersal. There are at least three hearths of seed plants, all forming strategically placed salients along climatic margins of the Old Planting area. All, I take it, began as gradual shifts of attention from cuttings to seeds, where environment became less favorable to root crops than to annual seed crops. This is again the thesis of the attractive volunteers. At the northeast, one complex of economic annuals took form in the loess country of China and perhaps in the mountain margins of inner China. A second was at the Ethiopian gateway to Africa. The third was in three segments: trans-Indus, cis-Indus, and the Near East, the last involving a shift from summer-rain to winter-rain crops. By their plant complexes, Ethiopia and China appear older than the central salient, and in the latter the Near East as later than the two sides of the Indus.

The dispersal of seed plants outlines certain far-reaching early lines of communication that may lie greatly beyond any times disclosed by the spade of the archeologist. The Indian–South Arabian–Abyssinian route of the Old Planting culture functioned again in the spread of seed agriculture and became extended in the opposite direction, through Upper Burma and Szechwan into the loess lands of North China. Along this line moved, from Africa, the sorghums, sesame, cowpeas, and the primordial cotton. The Chinese classical tradition is that sorghum came out of India within the Christian era. The botanical argument on the kaoliang races is to the contrary. Archeologically, Andersson has shown the Neolithic presence of rice culture in China[13] and Bishop has reported Neolithic kaoliang. Along this great way between Abyssinia and Shensi the seed annuals have left a trace of early civilization, inviting exploration (Pl. III).

The panic millets, if correctly credited to North China, indicate an early route diverging westward in India to pass into the Mediterranean and ultimately to the Iberian and Celtic peoples of the Atlantic.

The seed crops show a curious failure to disperse from Abyssinia down the Nile to Lower Egypt and into the Mediterranean. The sorghums, one of the most valuable lot of man-made plants, seem never to have taken hold to any extent in Lower Egypt or beyond. Pliny said that they were introduced in his lifetime from India. The Egyptians did not use cotton, which came west belatedly and slowly from India after Alexander's invasion. According to Burkill, the ancient African sesame reached Egypt about 1300 B. C. and, again, probably via India and Mesopotamia. The Abyssinian durum wheats seem not to have reached the Mediterranean until after Roman days. The block between Ethiopia and the Mediterranean was in part only climatic, between summer and winter growth seasons, gradually overcome by irrigation and the breeding of winter races. This is, however, obviously an inadequate explanation; an undisclosed cultural break is inferred that again invites study.

Herdsmen and Husbandmen

Herd Animals Belong with Seed Agriculture

The household animals I have associated with vegetative planting in origin; the herd animals belong with seed farming. The only exception is the reindeer, living in margins of the Arctic beyond the lands possible to cultivation. The notion that nomads domesticated herd animals stems from the age-old fancy that hunters became pastoralists and finally farmers, that hunters were the animal domesticators and that collectors learned how to grow plants. I know no evidence for such views, nor for the assumption underlying both, that growing scarcity of food gave the impetus to domestication. The dependence of the nomadic pastoralist on agricultural communities is well known and general, and his way of life is derived from the sedentary farmer.

The great thesis of the geographer Eduard Hahn needs some revision, but it has stood up remarkably for a half century. He started to write an economic geography and to map distributions of economic systems, but in order to explain geographic differences in gainful activities he found himself turning more and more to past conditions and so to the quest of agricultural origins. The query that really opened up to him the whole question of domestication was how, where, and why the milking of animals was begun. Having satisfied himself that pastoralism came out of agriculture and was practiced by people who lived on the margins of agriculture, he came to the con-

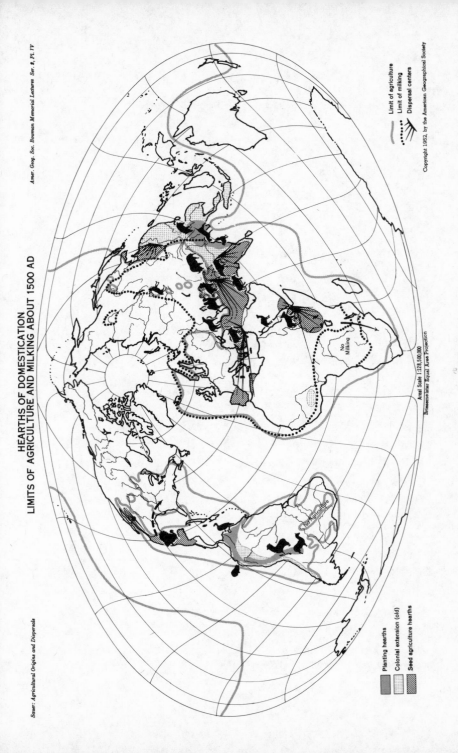

Sauer: *Agricultural Origins and Dispersals*

Amer. Geog. Soc. Bowman Memorial Lectures Ser. 2, Pl. IV

HEARTHS OF DOMESTICATION
LIMITS OF AGRICULTURE AND MILKING ABOUT 1500 AD

No Milking

No Agriculture

Limit of agriculture
Limit of milking
Dispersal centers

Copyright 1952, by the American Geographical Society

Areal Scale 1:128,500,000

Briesemeister Equal Area Projection

Planting hearths

Colonial extension (old)

Seed agriculture hearths

clusion that the herd animals were originally part of an early (he actually thought the earliest) seed agriculture, which arose in one particular region (he thought Mesopotamia). His views of place and time must be somewhat changed in the light of later evidence, but the domestication of herd animals by sedentary folk who were seed farmers and who arose out of one common way of life is still most acceptable, culturally and biologically.

The hearth of domestication of herd animals lies in Southwest Asia. To the myth of the wolf that became a dog by joining the campfire of hunters and the one that hungry collectors began to sow and thus originated the noble grains, we may add the fancy that enclosure of game animals by hunters was the means by which our herd animals came to be.

The bones of cattle, sheep, and goats are found with early village sites of seed farmers, dated as about seven thousand years old, and ranging from the base of the Cilician Mountains to the basin of Persepolis in south-central Persia.[1] Tell Hassuna in upper Mesopotamia and Tepe Sialk in central Persia, are among the oldest known. These records of the life and arts of ancient seed farmers and stock raisers exhibit conditions far removed from the beginnings of domestication, perhaps more different from their beginnings than they are from modern village life in the same parts. No more than for the crops has the archeologist discovered the beginnings of animal domestications, nor the order in which they appeared. For such reconstruction we must turn to the distribution of the wild forms, to bits of genetic evidence, all too few as yet about the descent of the domestic forms, and to folkways and folklore in different societies.

To confine bands of adult wild and lusty animals until they became domestic herd animals was not within the power of any early folk. The building of enclosures which could not be leaped or breached was hardly possible, nor was taming by starving into acceptance of food and obedience to man. Taming of the wild again may be thought of as beginning by infant capture, nursing by a foster mother, and raising the young in close association with man. I should start the procedure therefore in much the same manner as among the tropical planters, by fully sedentary folk, in this case seed farmers, who had no want of food and were not interested in the captured young as future roasts, but for entertainment or ceremonial. Pigs as well as dogs were already widely distributed, I have inferred as acquired from the planting cultures of the East. The pig, it should be remembered, was generally raised all across Southwest Asia and farther west until it became despised in the rise of newer religions. If any domestic mammals were already present, lactation of captured infant stock was simplified. A plausible reconstruction is thus: man returning from the hills with a kid or lamb, woman rearing it, and children growing up with the young animal and leading it out to browse. In such a gentle captivity, breeding might occur and thus domestication begin. In any case, hungry and errant hunters were not the ones who thought of domestication or could practice it.

Milking Common to Herd Animals

All the domestic herd animals are milked or have been thus used in the past. Milking may, therefore, have been both part of the process and purpose of their domestication. The wild forms of such animals are not more desirable sources of milk, either as to quality or amount, than a lot of other herbivores, accessible to man but never domesticated. Early in Hahn's study of economic geography he found that milking had a continuous distribution which could not be explained by climate, pasture, or anything else in the environment. Beyond this milking line there were people who had an aversion to milk and its products. In other words, here Hahn inferred a non-environmental culture trait that originated in one center and spread thence until stopped by other cultures that would have nothing to do with it. The original center, he judged correctly, lay in Southwest Asia. It was unknown in America, nor did the natives of the New World care for the strange practice when it was brought by the Europeans.

In the Old World, milking is not practiced in two agricultural areas, the Far East and the Pacific islands in Asia and the tropical forests of Africa.[2] Some of the animals milked elsewhere are kept in numbers and of old both in the Orient and inner Africa. The explanation that the Chinese do not use milk because they got cattle and goats before milking was invented is an assumption unsupported by any evidence. I think it more likely that the Orientals and central Africans accepted some domesticated herd animals, but did not take on the habit of milking because it was strange to their ways and they did not like it. We know that the Orient remained in communication with Southwest Asia and that there was continuing transfer of ideas that were congenial. The cultures that rejected milking were the two ancient planting cultures, and the basis of rejection is probably only antipathy.

That milking began for economic ends is, I think, also unlikely. At the beginning of domestication, the animals secreted milk enough only for their young, or very little more. That small children might on occasion share milk of goat or ewe with the animal young is hardly a sufficient basis for starting a milking economy.

[87]

Ceremonial Basis of Domestication

In the domestication of the herd animals, religious ideas, concerned with the origin of life, are deeply involved. Hahn came to the conclusion, and thereby gave offense to some of his colleagues, that these animals were desired and used by man first for ceremonial purposes, in particular in connection with fertility cults. In the lands from India to the Mediterranean there is a substratum of primordial religions, pre-Indo-European and pre-Semitic earth gods, spirits of wood and water of pantheistic or animistic nature. There was especially about the eastern end of the Mediterranean from very olden times a cult of the Magna Mater, or Earth Goddess, who became Ishtar, Astarte, Demeter or some other goddess of later religions. These seem to have walked the earth for a long while before they became heavenly deities. In their earlier forms they had in themselves the power of procreation; as virgin goddesses they brought fertility to field and flock. The Eleusinian mysteries, celebrating Demeter, seem to have had no sexuality, certainly nothing of religious orgies. The principle of fertility was in the female, the male was irrelevant or subordinate.

Later, the Great Mother seems to have become a moon goddess, and also the religions became heterosexual and acquired ceremonies that were orgiastic. Fertility rituals became dramatically realistic and obsessive. And then the time of the paternal, dominant gods had arrived. Finally sex was exorcised by the rise of monotheism and theology based on ethics. I am apologetic about this extreme simplification of one of the most difficult questions in our cultural backgrounds. It is, however, also one of the most important ones and Hahn was right in seeing ceremonial bases in the keeping of herd animals.[3] The materialism of our time assumes that consciously direct economic motives are the mainspring of human inventiveness.

This projection of ourselves into a remote past may greatly misinterpret motives, ends, and means.

An elder maternal society does underlie the high cultures of the ancient West. In it we may expect to find the beginnings of milking domestication. Again, the Canaries give a glimpse of what may have been. According to the old accounts, the people were matrilineally organized, and had, in the terms of the chroniclers, queens, high priestesses, and prophetesses. Milk and butter appear to have been the only offerings made in their ceremonies.[4]

By the time religion and society were paternally reorganized in the lands of the old western civilization sacrificial killing of animals had become high ceremony. The offerings were of domestic animals with preference as to kind by particular divinities. Hahn saw in these cult associations of god and animal the main cause of domestication. The sacrifice was partaken of by priests, the elite, and perhaps the commoners. Sacred uses became profane as old meanings and reverences became blurred and the meats of cult festivals became the food of those who could afford it. The originally sacred animal became homely and utilitarian, not the other way around.

We incline to overstress slaughtered meat in the diet of the early husbandmen. Proteins and fats rather were mainly from plant sources. "Esau was a cunning hunter, a man of the field; and Isaac loved Esau, because he did eat of his venison." Yet when Esau returned hungry, he sold his birthright for "bread and pottage of lentiles." The order of importance may have been thus: pulses first, game next, and slaughtered meat last. There were many kinds of game; the hunt even in times of high civilization continued to be a major source of meat. It was often and for a long time cheaper to get meat by hunting than by raising it. I doubt that we produce more meat today on ranges than wild game would yield from the same land. Beef in particular never seems to have been an ordinary meat anywhere in the Near East or the Mediterranean.

Domestication as to Kind

The kinds of animals that were domesticated are curious and meaningful. There was high diversity of game animals in the Levant and its borderlands: antelopes and gazelles in the plains; wild cattle, bison, and buffalo in forest, brush, and grassland; deer of various kinds and habits; goats and sheep in rocky and mountainous lands; camels in deserts; horses and asses in continuous distribution from the Cape of Good Hope north to the Siberian taiga. Of this multitude only a very few were domesticated, though the ancient sculptures and paintings abound in hunting scenes of diverse sorts and also tell of the keeping of numerous kinds tamed.

The selection was not based on propinquity to man, nor on sharing his habitat. It was not based on declining abundance, for most of the domestication took place near the margins of the natural range occupied by the species. It was not based on docility: antelopes, gazelles, and deer, easily tamed and much kept for diversion, provided no domesticate except the reindeer. This animal of the cold north seems to be a belated substitute added when pastoralism spread into the margins of the Arctic.[5] Rather, one might say that animals were chosen for domestication that were not easy to take, which were not common, and which were difficult to make gentle—the wild mountain goats and sheep that avoid the vicinity of man, the formidable wild cattle and buffalo. Hunting the urus (*Bos primigenius*) was a sport of major hazard and elaborate organization to the time of their extinction in the seventeenth century of our era. Yet this is the ancestor of our domestic cattle. The feared wild cattle of India, the gaur, are no more dangerous than was the urus. The Old World bison, a very near relative of our American bison, never had such a reputation for ferocity. It occupied a very great range that extended well into the lands of ancient civilization. It was desirable for meat, hide and wool, but no domestication was undertaken; the failure to do so was not due to its nature, habitat, or economic suitability.

The eleven domesticates are: the common cattle, zebu, water buffalo, yak, goat, sheep, reindeer, dromedary, Bactrian camel, horse, and ass, all now or once milch animals. Except the reindeer, all are first known from ancient seed-agricultural centers and their wild ranges are in or marginal to such areas. The coincidence of the west Asiatic centers of seed domestication and of herd animals is such that they appear as complementary features of one cultural complex (Pl. III).

Goats and Sheep

The goat may possibly begin the series of herd domestications. It has been distributed all the way across Eurasia and to the south end of Africa, penetrating both the non-milking cultures of the Far East and of tropical Africa quite generally. Among African forest folk it is often the most important domestic animal, especially a dwarf race which has been thought to be akin to the turbary Neolithic goat of Swiss lake dwellers. There are very many domestic races in the Old World and they have not been well studied. It is probable that the blood of several wild species has been introduced into the domestic forms, but the main descent is traced from the southwest Asiatic bezoar goat (*Capra aegagrus*), a mountain animal ranging west of the Indus to the Caucasus. Adametz thought the earliest pictorial representations in the Near East to be a domestic version of the screw horned *C. falconeri,* native to the western Himalayas, Afghanistan, and east Bukhara, and known to be fully fertile in crosses with the house goat.[6] First choice as to place of origin therefore goes to the cis-Indus country (Area B of the seed hearths). The wild forms live in the mountains well above, but at no great distance from the ancient agricultural valleys.

Culturally there are a number of suggestions of high antiquity. The goat is both herd and household animal and is found among people who have none of the other herd animals, but who keep pigs and fowls. It is sacrificed, but usually as second choice to sheep. Goat gods, such as Pan, and the ritual scapegoat, may be traits of degradation such as elder gods and elder rites have often suffered.

Sheep were domesticated in the same general area as the goat, the chief parent being considered *Ovis vignei*. Adametz ties an early domestic form with horizontal spiral horns to a variety of *O. vignei* living from the Salt Range of the Punjab to Baluchistan, emphasizing "the outstanding role which these parts of Asia played, in part as centers of origin, in part as staging areas of domestic animals and peoples in the early history of mankind, moving from East to West." Independently, therefore, the seed plants of Area B and sheep and goats have been assigned to the same area as to domestic hearths, from which they passed into the Near East and beyond. Fat tails and woolly fleeces were later developments of domestication. In Ethiopia parallel selection formed races of goats and sheep so much alike as to confuse travellers and lead to stories of crosses between the two.

The Ass

The ass was the lone contribution of Africa to the domesticated animals. An equally attractive lot of wild asses, half asses, and zebras held contiguous ranges from extreme southern Africa across the Near East and Turkestan into north-central

Asia, but only one form, the wild ass of Nubia, was domesticated. Its origin is, therefore, in association with that of the great group of economic annuals formed in the same area, Ethiopia. It is the original pack animal of the old civilizations and probably the earliest riding animal. Its breeding was not directed, as it readily could have been, toward the development of draft power. The use of its milk is now mostly restricted to cosmetics, medicine, and magic.

Cattle

The original ceremonial domestication of cattle was proposed by Hahn to much academic headshaking. In brief, they were, in his view, the originally sacred animals in the moon cult, their horns symbolizing the crescent moon. Milking and castration were fertility rituals. Sacred oxen first drew the ceremonial cart and pulled the plow, a phallic symbol for the insemination of the receptive earth. Cattle, cart, plow, broadcasting, and drilling all began as ceremonies of a rising fertility cult of the Near East in which the officiants were males, and henceforth the care of the cattle, the hand at the plow, the sower, was male. The husbandman thereafter takes over the agricultural operations, the women retire to the house and to garden work. Paternal societies are formed, with priests and kings, politics and states, aristocracies and subjects. The male hierarchies prevailed where cattle, plowed fields, and wagons became dominant institutions. The thesis was repugnant to materialistic rationalism. It also offended because it placed sex at the center of esoteric religious matters. It remains a great contribution, still acceptable in large part.

The ancestral wild stock is one species complex, *Bos primigenius* in the west, from Atlantic Europe into western Asia, *Bos namadicus* in India. These wild cattle, among the strongest and most savage of game animals, held their own against all predators, and there seems to be no record of their being broken or tamed as adults. Both domestic types appear near the beginning of the archeological record of agriculture, common cattle in upper Mesopotamia at Tell Hassuna, the zebu at Rana Ghundai I in north Baluchistan. At such early time this part of the world was permeated by the Great-Mother cult, followed later by the moon goddess. The earliest ceremonial carts were drawn by oxen; there is even an early figurine in which a goddess sits on a throne on an ox-drawn sled.[7] Priests officiated at ceremonial plowing, of phallic symbolism. Cattle were the plow animals exclusively for a long time; their economic use for milk was less than of other animals and production for beef was never important in the older lands. Milking and meat raising became dominant on later peripheries, in northern Europe and east Africa.

The Camels

Camels were on the verge of extinction when they became domesticated. No wild dromedaries have ever been known, and prevailing zoologic opinion considers the living "wild" two-humped camels of Chinese Turkestan as feral. The dromedary is linked with Semitic peoples and an Arabian domestication is commonly assumed. There are a few early Egyptian representations, none, it is said, being known after the First Dynasty until the time of the Ptolemies.[8] This early Egyptian knowledge suggests a center in western Arabia, where quite early agricultural settlements may be inferred, though such have not been proven. The spread of the dromedary was late and then rather rapid when states and trade required a transport animal for desert crossings. For the Bactrian camel, no other locality is indicated than the one that gives the name. A separate domestication is inferred because crosses with the dromedary are sterile. Such hybrids were fairly common in Asia Minor in classical times, where it is thought also that the breeding of mules originated. Neither dromedary nor Bactrian need be assigned to nomad origin. Bactria is a farming land more ancient than the probable time of camel domestication. So too, it is surmised, is Yemen, and probably Hejaz; there are botanical indications that point that way.

The Horse

The horse has been well studied by comparative zoology and is referred to tarpan ancestry.[9] This wild horse, extinct only a few decades ago, ranged the south Russian steppes to the Caucasus. Crossings of tarpan stock and the heavier forest breeds of western Europe may have produced the big-boned draft horses. Lately we have learned that the domestic horse was known to the ancient civilizations in the third millenium B. C., as at Harappa on the Indus, Rana Ghundai in Baluchistan, in the second phase of Sialk in Persia, early Anau, and pre-dynastic Mesopotamia.[10] It may be inferred that horses in small numbers were carried southeastward from the margins of the Caucasus a thousand years before the animal became important in the ancient civilizations. This time is notably earlier than anything known about Indo-European peoples. Some unknown people, probably sedentary farmers, I should say, at the northern base of the Caucasus, effected the domestication.

Historically the horse is associated mainly with the Indo-European migrations, martial bands that poured across Anatolia into the Fertile Crescent, through Media into India, and out of the Russian plains into the Mediterranean peninsulas and western Europe. With the horse came the war chariot and the cavalryman, new forms of war and conquest, military aristocracy. To Indo-Europeans it was the animal of prestige, the sacred animal above all others, the high sacrifice, the flesh of solemn festivals. To the nomads of interior Asia it became the provider of fermented milk, kumiss. To our ancestors it was a source of meat, though much less so than were beeves. Christianity stamped out the eating of horseflesh among our people since it was a main link to pagan ways.

Restatement of Culture Periods

The naming of the great cultural time divisions by stone and metal stresses minor attainments of man. Restatement changes the emphasis thus:

The Neolithic opens with well-established agriculture, and a rather full complement of the crops and animals still basic to the Old World. The great, long, and tedious job of domestication was done before then. For western civilization the common center was a series of mountain-margined basins from the Indus Valley west to the Levant.

At the end of the Neolithic, plow agriculture becomes dominant and powerful states develop. As a rough marker we may use a time around 3000 B. C. when dynasties appear. In this change, the supremacy of the male becomes established and new religions arise; the moon goddess becomes subordinate to the Sun God, her crescent ultimately the symbol of Allah.

Around a thousand years later the great historic peoples take the center of the stage, first Semites, then Hamites and Indo-Europeans. Their ancestors may have lived on the fringes of the older, unnamed agriculturists, perhaps as hunters and collectors who gradually learned the arts of tillage and stockraising. Their contributions are in political organization and the setting up of codes of law, in war and conquest, in cities and commerce, and in time as makers of theologies and philosophies, the usual stuff of history.

Separation of Herdsmen from Husbandmen

The separation of herdsman from husbandman came about insensibly and imperfectly. "Abel was a keeper of sheep, but Cain was a tiller of the ground," and both were of one family. Beyond the tilled lands of the villagers lay the open range where herds grazed or browsed in hills and mountains and on plains too dry to farm. In the off season, the fallow fields provided additional grazing. Feed from browse was important, probably more so than grass. As the numbers of people and stock increased, herdsmen and herd moved farther and farther away from the villages and became more permanently detached from the settled lands. This about describes the roots of pastoral nomadism. As with village Arab and Bedouin, sedentary folk and mobile tent dwellers are mostly one people. In Inner Asia, earlier hunting peoples took on herd animals from other kinds of folk to the south, but still there is some dependence of herdsman on farmer for grain. The original and absolute pastoralists can scarcely be said to exist or ever to have existed; they derive from a farming culture in which livestock was an original element.

Hamitic and Indo-European migrations were largely driven by a strong bent toward herding. The former, stemming out of a common background with the Semites, moved across north and east Africa, bearers of a cattle culture in which the beasts were — and are — prized far beyond their economic utility. Hamitic cattle lords spread over the native hoe-tilling peoples in a sort of symbiosis in which the privileged group were masters of the cattle, the peasant mass grew the field crops. The

[97]

Aryan invasion of India had similar aristocratic quality. In Europe successive Indo-European waves overran and mingled with the older sedentary cultivators. The latter are still partially recognizable in "Mediterranean" racial stocks in the south and west and Alpines in the central mountains and hill lands. Some of the Indo-European bands came by way of Asia Minor, others by way of the Russian plains, all with their herds of cattle and horses.

North European Husbandry

Our forebears, drifting west and north, got into lands of shorter and cooler summers and of mixed forests or woodlands. The farther they went the more did climate restrict their habits. By the time they settled on the Baltic and North Sea lowlands, they were stockmen, not cultivators. Studies of pollen that drifted into bogs have enabled a pretty accurate reconstruction of vegetation.[11] The earliest clearing of land was not for sown fields but for pastures and meadows; the newly-immigrated plants were only pasture weeds. Somewhat later, the first grains appear, wheat and barley; still later, rye and oats. The pollen record is checked by seed impressions in potsherds of known age.[12]

Rye and, in part, oats are wild grasses at home in western Asia, mingling in fields with wheat and barley but only as weeds. Primitive methods of harvest and winnowing did not separate weed seed from grain and so the ryes and oats marched along with the wheat and barley in their westward travels. Meanwhile, a partial domestication had taken place quite by chance, for the strains of rye and oats that remained intermingled with the cultivated grains were those that had become non-shattering, matured at the same time as the cultivated plants, had similar grain and stalk sizes, and hence became part

[98]

of the harvested crop. As the growing of cereals spread into lands of colder and wetter summers and acid soils, barley and in particular wheat did less and less well, the volunteer rye and oats relatively better and in the end these became the cultivated crops and the north Atlantic lands came to depend on them for human cereal.

Thus arose a distinctive farming system north of the Alps and west of the Russian steppes. This was a balanced, mixed farming, primarily an animal husbandry. Milk products were most important and, with dairying, the calf crop increased the meat supply. Clearing of new ground was primarily to gain more pasture and meadow. The limiting factor always was the amount of feed that could be grown for the animals, the grazing available during open weather, the hay that could be stored against winter. This economy produced the barn for hay and the stable for stock. Field crops took second place to hay crop. Rye had increased importance because, being fall sown, it provided some winter pasture. Fertility was maintained because the stable manure was returned to the fields. Long continued pasturing and mowing selected an association of forage plants that prospered under the bite of cattle and cut of scythe in a closed ecologic cycle, as Gradmann liked to point out. Man took from the ground no more than he returned; he did not lose topsoil by overcultivation nor was it lost to winter rains. Production was not at a high level, nor was the life of the husbandman easy, but man lived durably on the land and could expect his descendants to do so.

Such were the systems of culture across northwestern Europe for two to three thousand years, systems not seriously modified until the eighteenth century. Then, with the introduction of the potato, the development of stock beets and field turnips, and the cultivation of clovers, the new agricultural revolution arose and, in part, prepared the way for the industrial revolution.

The Problem of Desiccation

In lands of uncertain or markedly seasonal rainfall the tenure of man has often been insecure. The ruins of settled communities are strewn across the heart of the Old World from the Tarim Basin of Inner Asia to Mauritania on the Atlantic shore of Africa. The land has become desolate where fields long were tilled and flocks and herds grazed. Within the dry lands and all about them human occupation has broken down from time to time over a long period and there has been progressive shrinkage of the habitable land. Neolithic settlements are found where no later villages were built; Roman colonies thrived where now are only occasional herdsmen; medieval settlements failed in their turn.

Thus it has become customary to speak of the 'desiccation' of the heart of the Old World as an ancient and continuing process. The Sahara in particular is said to be extending year by year. One school of thought asserts long continued climatic deterioration. Ellsworth Huntington, who had taken part in the exploration of the ruins of Anau, devoted much of his life to the thesis that the dry climates are growing drier and more extensive. Many archeologists, especially British, accept increasing aridity as a principal cause of failure of settlements. On the other hand it may not be necessary to postulate a change in the mechanism of atmospheric circulation to account for the human failures, but to explain these by the action of man.

It seems to me there has been misconstruction of various data. It has been too freely assumed that loss of vegetation and fauna must be the result of climatic change. Climatic data from northern Europe have been misapplied to distant and different situations. Especially is this true of the so-called "climatic optimum." About the Baltic and North Sea bog studies have shown a series of vegetational changes, rather closely identified as to time. For a period when certain plants, such as ivy, mistletoe, and oak grew farther north than at present the term "climatic optimum" was introduced to express some increase in length or warmth of summer. This phrase has been picked up by students of the ancient Near East and applied there incautiously. No one has explained how the factor of summer temperature in Scandinavia becomes a matter of moisture in the Near East. A misunderstood phrase has beguiled and bemused.

The early and long recurrent failures of settlements have happened in areas subject to marked variability of rainfall. In good years they have enough water; in others they suffer. The margins of the dry lands have always been hazardous to man. His own numbers and those of his flocks increase to full use of optimal weather conditions; a run of dry years brings overgrazing, depletion of the more palatable plants, baring of surface to wash and wind. Man tries as long as he can to counter the natural checks on population that tend to restore ecologic balance. The result is that after a time of weather stress the land does not recover its former ability to grow useful plant cover and to absorb moisture. In our short occupation of our dry West, we have ample experience of ecologic deterioration, as by successive drops in range capacity through a series of droughts. These man-made pressures have existed in the Old World a hundred times as long as with us. Maintenance of human and animal numbers as close to normal or optimal moisture conditions as possible brings recurrent and increasing imbalance and surface attrition, which may resemble the effects of increased aridity.

There are significant contrasts in surface and vegetation between our dry lands and those of the Old World. Ours, except the most extreme, are fairly well vegetated and carry a richly diverse flora. The Sonoran desert, meteorologically quite similar to the western Sahara, is an impressive display of bloom in spring and early summer, with abundant insect, bird, and rodent life, mule deer, antelope, mountain sheep—a rewarding collecting ground for the naturalist. It has no lifeless spaces, in contrast to the wastes of climatically similar areas in the Old World.

We have no great expanses of moving sand or rock-surfaced hammadas. Aside from the Peruvian desert, where the sand dunes are mainly derivative from sea beaches, our dune belts, as along the lower Colorado and in Chihuahua, are Pleistocene relics of pluvial periods when former lakes and stream floods provided sand in beaches and bars. Despite the greater aridity of the present these dunes have become fixed by vegetation except where they are disturbed by man. If climatic change is responsible for the "desiccation" of the Old World, similar effects should be equally apparent in the New World. I have been more than a casual student of our dry areas for years and in different parts, and I know of no such late modification of climates.

The difference between the deserts and their margins in the Old and the New Worlds may be explained by the different histories of occupation by man. The Old World lands were lived in much longer by more people and by people who turned flocks and herds out to graze and browse. The people of the New World had neither herd animals nor plow. Not only Spanish exploring parties but United States military and railroad surveys in our Southwest provide evidence that less than a century of grazing and plowing has greatly modified and reduced the vegetation, precariously balanced in ecologic tension zones of frequent droughts. The Old World also has, especially in the eastern half of the Mediterranean and the Near East, a great deal of limestone country, attractive for cultivation and productive of good forage, but vulnerable to erosion as limestone lands are, because soil is likely to be underlain at shallow depth by solid rock. The bare limestone ribs of Mother Earth whiten the slopes of many of the uplands of the ancient civilizations where once lay good fields and fat pastures. I should attach first importance therefore to the cumulative effects of soil erosion, through thousands of years. Across the heart of the Old World neither herdsman nor plowman was able to maintain a lasting position for himself in an environment of recurrent droughts. The land became more and more bared to wash and wind. Man has been long in retreat before the growing desert he has helped to make. The desert continues to grow, not because of progressive deterioration of climate but because of continuing attrition of cover and surface.

––––––––––

We are at the end of this summary review of what man has done with the plants and animals at his disposal. His mastery over the organic world began with his employment of and experiments with fire. Sedentary fishing peoples perhaps commenced the cultivation of plants and became the first domesticators of plants and animals. The earliest plant selection was by vegetative reproduction and the early domestic animals were part of the household. Later came plant selection by seed reproduction and the keeping of flocks by seed farmers. I have thought to link these inventions in series, possibly beginning from a common center, and to follow their dispersals and divergences. If this be exaggeration of the processes of diffusion of learning, the proposed thesis may be taken as an invitation to study the various lines of evidence as to the growth of the agricultural arts.

Our civilization still rests, and will continue to rest, on the discoveries made by peoples for the most part unknown to history. Historic man has added no plant or animal of major importance to the domesticated forms on which he depends. He has learned lately to explain a good part of the mechanisms of selection, but the arts thereof are immemorial and represent an achievement that merits our respect and attention. We remain a part of the organic world, and as we intervene more and more decisively to change the balance and nature of life, we have also more need to know, by retrospective study, the responsibilities and hazards of our present and our prospects as lords of creation.

GENERAL REFERENCES AND NOTES

The following selected general references, listed by topic, are given for the reader who may be interested in knowing some of my major guides. Our geographers have little awareness of the great handbooks relevant to their work: here are some of them. References to specific points in the text follow under chapter headings.

SELECTED GENERAL REFERENCES

On Plants

Oakes Ames: Economic Annuals and Human Cultures, *Botan. Museum Harvard Univ.*, Cambridge, Mass., 1939.

Edgar Anderson: Plants, Man and Life, Boston, 1952. Recommended for parallel reading. An engaging, learned, and original account of the ways in which plants are changed by association with man, especially by hybridization.

D. Bois: Les plantes alimentaires chez tous peuples et à travers les âges, Paris, 1927, ff.

D. C. Darlington and E. K. Janaki: Chromosome Atlas of Cultivated Plants, London, 1950.

A. Engler and K. Prantl: Die natürlichen Pflanzenfamilien, Leipzig, 1887–1915.

R. Gradmann: Hackbau und Kulturpflanzen, *Deutsches Archiv für Landes und Volksforschung*, Vol. 6, Leipzig, 1942.

A. G. Haudricourt and Louis Hédin: L'homme et les plantes cultivées, Paris, 1943.

Elisabeth Schiemann: Entstehung der Kulturpflanzen (Handbuch der Vererbungswissenschaft), Berlin, 1932.

N. I. Vavilov: The Origin, Variation, Immunity and Breeding of Cultivated Plants: Translated from the Russian by K. Starr Chester, *Chronica Botanica*, Vol. 13, Nos. 1–6, 1949–1950.

On Animals

Leopold Adametz: Herkunft und Wanderungen der Hamiten, Vienna, 1920.

Brehm: Tierleben, 10th edit., 1920. Especially for Max Hilzheimer's contributions on domestic forms and their wild kindred.

Ernst Feige: Die Haustierzonen der alten Welt, *Petermanns Ergänzungsheft* 198, 1928.

B. Klatt: Entstehung der Haustiere (Handbuch der Vererbungswissenschaft), Berlin, 1927.

Regional Handbooks (All are more inclusive than titles indicate)

> *India.* George Watt: The Commercial Products of India, London, 1908; *idem:* A Dictionary of the Economic Products of India, 7 vols., Calcutta, 1889–1896.
> T. H. Engelbrecht: Die Feldfrüchte Indiens in ihrer geographischen Verbreitung, Hamburg, 1914.
> *Southeast Asia.* I. H. Burkill: A Dictionary of the Economic Products of the Malay Peninsula, London, 1935.
> K. Heyne: De nuttige planten van Nederlandsch Indië, new edit., Buitenzorg, 1927.
> *Africa.* F. Stuhlmann: Beiträge zur Kulturgeschichte von Ostafrika, Berlin, 1909.
> H. Baumann, R. Thurnwald, and D. Westermann: Völkerkunde von Afrika, Essen, 1940.

Culture History and Geography

Max Ebert (ed.): Reallexikon der Vorgeschichte, 15 vols., Berlin, 1924–1932. Invaluable for articles by specialists (includes latest views of Eduard Hahn and Max Hilzheimer).

Eduard Hahn: Die Haustiere und ihre Beziehungen zum Menschen, Leipzig, 1896; *idem:* Die Entstehung der Pflugkultur, Heidelberg, 1909; *idem:* Von der Hacke zum Pflug, Leipzig, 1914. See also the "Festschrift" to Hahn, Stuttgart, 1917.

Iwan v. Müller (ed.): Handbuch der (Klassischen) Altertumswissenschaft, 1885, ff.

Karl Sapper: Geographie und Geschichte der indianischen Landwirtschaft, Hamburg, 1936.

NOTE ON THE MAPS

The maps are attempts to reconstruct the hearths of domestication and the routes by which the ideas and objects of agriculture were spread. Maps are likely to carry even more assurance of knowledge than do texts; the reader is warned that Plates I to IV attempt only to set forth what is, as of present knowledge, reasonable interpretation. They are work sheets to be revised as better knowledge comes to hand of the evolution of man's plants and animals, of their remains recovered in archeology, of their implications in different cultures, of the climates, shore lines, and land surfaces of the prehistoric human past. The earliest design on which they are based is Vavilov's map of World Centers of Origin of Cultivated Plants (*op. cit.*, pp. 23–24), revised by Darlington and Janaki (first end piece of Chromosome Atlas). In the present set of maps, additional plant data have been used, domestic animals related to plant domestication, and inferences made as to cultural dispersals.

The maps were drawn by John Philip of the American Geographical Society's cartographic staff. Plate II uses the bipolar conformal conic projection designed by O. M. Miller (see *Geogr. Rev.*, Vol. 31, 1941), Plate IV, the equal area projection designed by William Briesemeister for the Society's "Atlas of Distribution of Diseases."

NOTES ON THE BOWMAN LECTURES

Chapter I

[1] Marston Bates: Where Winter Never Comes, New York, 1952. A biologist considers the tropics in relation to human cultures.

[2] G. C. Simpson: World Climate during the Quaternary Period, *Quart. Journ. Royal Meteorol. Soc.*, Vol. 60, 1934, pp. 425–478.

Idem: Possible Causes of Changes of Climate and Their Limitations, *Proc. Linnean Soc.*, Vol. 152, 1940, pp. 190–219.

H. C. Willett: Solar Variability as a Factor in the Fluctuations of Climate during Geological Time, *in* Glaciers and Climate, *Geogr. Annaler*, Vol. 31, No. 1–2, 1949, pp. 295–315. (Geophysical and geomorphological essays dedicated to Hans W:son Ahlmann.)

J. B. Leighly: On Continentality and Glaciation, *ibid.*, pp. 134–145.

[3] F. E. Zeuner: Dating the Past, 2nd edit. rev., London, 1950. Gives comparative data on distributions of Pleistocene man by time and area.

[4] A. Penck: Wann kamen die Indianer nach Nordamerika?, *Proc. 23rd Internatl. Congr. of Americanists, New York, 1928*, New York, 1930, pp. 23–30.

G. F. Carter: Man in America: A Criticism of Scientific Thought, *Scientific Monthly*, Vol. 73, 1951, pp. 297–307.

[5] This is in terms of the Simpson glacial hypothesis and by referring the period of the Alaskan "deep thaw" to that time. See C. O. Sauer: A Geographic Sketch of Early Man in America, *Geogr. Rev.*, Vol. 34, 1944, pp. 529–573, esp. pp. 532–535.

[6] L. Stewart: Burning and Natural Vegetation in the United States, *Geogr. Rev.*, Vol. 41, 1951, pp. 317–320.

[7] C. O. Sauer: Early Relations of Man to Plants, *Geogr. Rev.*, Vol. 37, 1947, pp. 1–25.

[8] C. O. Sauer: Grassland Climax, Fire, and Man, *Journ. of Range Management*, Vol. 3, 1950, pp. 16–21.

[9] W. S. Cooper: The Broadleaf-Sclerophyll Vegetation of California, *Carnegie Instn. of Washington Publ. No. 319*, 1922.

[10] C. O. Sauer: Geography of the Pennyroyal, *Kentucky Geol. Survey*, Ser. 6, Vol. 25, Frankfort, Ky., 1927.

[11] Ames, *op. cit.* [see Gen. Refs.]

Chapter II

[1] C. O. Sauer: American Agricultural Origins: A Consideration of Nature and Culture, *in* Essays in Anthropology in Honor of A. L. Kroeber, University of California Press, 1936; ref. on p. 279.

[2] Grahame Clark: Farmers and Forests in Neolithic Europe, *Antiquity*, Vol. 19, 1946, pp. 57–71.

[3] C. O. Sauer: Cultivated Plants of South and Central America, *in* Handbook of South American Indians, *Bur. of Amer. Ethnology Bull. 143*, Vol. 6, pp. 487–543.

[4] C. O. Sauer: Environment and Culture during the Last Deglaciation, *Proc. Amer. Philosoph. Soc.*, Vol. 92, 1948, pp. 65–77.

[5] E. E. Cheesman: On the Nomenclature of Edible Bananas, *Journ. of Genetics*, Vol. 48, 1948, pp. 293–296.

[6] Burkill, *op. cit.* [see Gen. Refs.]. The main cultural conclusions of his taxonomic studies of the yam genus are incorporated.

Idem: The Rise and Decline of the Greater Yam in the Service of Man, *The Advancement of Science*, Vol. 7, 1951, pp. 443–448.

[7] Haudricourt and Hédin, *op. cit.* [see Gen. Refs.]; ref. on p. 153.

[8] E. Dahr: Studien über Hunde aus primitiven Steinzeitkulturen in Nordeuropa, *Lunds Univ. Arsskrift*, N. S. Sect. 2, Vol. 32, No. 4, 1937. Dahr has summarized the earlier studies in the comparative anatomy of dog and kindred.

[9] Freda Kretschmar: Hundestammvater und Kerberos, 2 vols., Stuttgart, 1938.

[10] C. W. Bishop: The Neolithic Age in Northern China, *Antiquity*, Vol. 7, 1933, pp. 389–404.

[11] B. Dürigen: Die Geflügelzucht, Berlin, 1923; ref. on p. 224.

[12] C. S. Coon: Southern Arabia: A Problem for the Future, *in* Papers Peabody Museum of Amer. Archeol. and Ethnol., Harvard Univ., Vol. 20 (Dixon Memorial Vol.), 1943, pp. 187–220.

[13] O. Menghin: Weltgeschichte der Steinzeit, Vienna, 1931.

[14] On domestic forms of pig, see Klatt,˙*op. cit.* [see Gen. Refs.].

[15] D. J. Wölfel: Leonardo Torriani, Die Kanarischen Inseln und ihre Urbewohner, Eine unbekannte Bilderhandschrift vom Jahre 1590, Leipzig, 1940; ref. on pp. 188–189.

Chapter III

[1] Sauer: American Agricultural Origins, *op. cit.*; ref. on p. 270.

[2] Ames, *op. cit.* [see Gen. Refs.]; ref. on pp. 44–49.

[3] R. M. Gilmore: Fauna and Ethnozoology of South America, *in* Handbook of South American Indians, *Bur. of Amer. Ethnology Bull. 143*, Vol. 6, 1950, pp. 345–464; ref. on pp. 370–373.

[4] J. G. Hawkes: Potato Collecting Expeditions in Mexico and South America, Imperial Bureau of Plant Breeding and Genetics, Cambridge, England, 1944.

[5] W. E. Castle and S. Wright: Studies of Inheritance in Guinea Pigs and Rats, *Carnegie Instn. of Washington Publ. 241*, 1916.

[6] R. E. Latcham: Arqueología de la region Atacameña, Santiago, 1938.

[7] Gilmore, *op. cit.*

[8] Erland Nordenskiöld: Deductions Suggested by the Geographical Distribution of Some Post-Columbian Words Used by the Indians of South America, Comparative Ethnographic Studies, Vol. 5, Göteborg, 1922. Chapters I and II, pp. 1–46, are on the domestic fowl.

[9] R. E. Latcham: Animales domésticos de la America pre-Colombiana, Santiago, 1922.

[10] R. C. Punnett: The Blue Egg, *Journ. of Genetics*, Vol. 17, 1933, pp. 465–470.

[11] Junius Bird: America's Oldest Farmers, *Natural History*, Vol. 57, 1948, pp. 296–303 and 334–345.

[12] J. B. Hutchinson, R. A. Silow, and S. G. Stephens: The Evolution of Gossypium, Oxford University Press, 1947; also the article by S. G. Stephens: Cytogenetics of Gossypium and the Problem of the Origin of New World Cottons, *Advances in Genetics*, Vol. 1, 1947, pp. 431–442. See the review by George F. Carter, *Geogr. Rev.*, Vol. 38, 1948, pp. 167–169.

Chapter IV

[1] G. F. Carter: An Early American Description Probably Referring to *Phaseolus lunatus*, *Chronica Botanica*, Vol. 12, 1951, pp. 155–160.

[2] T. W. Whitaker and J. B. Bird: Identification and Significance of the Cucurbit Materials from Huaca Prieta, Peru, *Amer. Museum Novitates*, No. 1426, 1949.

[3] D. Bois, *op. cit.* [see Gen. Refs.].

[4] T. W. Whitaker: A Species Cross in Cucurbita, *Journ. of Heredity*, Vol. 42, 1951, pp. 65–69.

[5] T. W. Whitaker and G. W. Bohn: Taxonomy, Genetics, Production and Uses of the Cultivated Species of Cucurbita, *Econ. Botany*, Vol. 4, 1950, pp. 52–81.

[6] A. Starker Leopold: The Wild Turkeys of Mexico, *Trans. 13th North Amer. Wildlife Conference*, Washington, 1948, pp. 393–400.

[7] Bishop, *op. cit.;* ref. on p. 395.

[8] Vavilov, *op. cit.* [see Gen. Refs.]; ref. on p. 38.

[9] E. Schiemann: New Results on the History of Cultivated Cereals, *Heredity*, Vol. 5, 1951, pp. 305–320.

[10] Hutchinson, Silow, and Stephens, *op. cit.*

[11] See Edgar Anderson [Gen. Refs.] for the latest, and in some ways differing, version of wheat origins. The book was received too late to be utilized in this text.

[12] Stuart Piggott: Prehistoric India to 1000 B. C., Pelican Books, Harmondsworth, England, 1950; ref. on pp. 46–48.

[13] J. Gunnar Andersson: Children of the Yellow Earth: Studies in Prehistoric China, New York, 1934.

Chapter V

[1] See Pl. III, facing p. 74, and data in Stuart Piggott, *op. cit.*

[2] For the determination of the latter area, I am indebted to Fred Simoons, Dept. of Geography, University of California, Berkeley.

[3] This is accepted by Klatt in his study of the genetics of animal domestication.

[4] D. J. Wölfel, *op. cit.;* ref. on pp. 79, 115, 240.

[5] N. T. Mirov: Notes on the Domestication of Reindeer, *Amer. Anthropologist*, Vol. 47, 1945, pp. 393–408. I am also indebted to him for the delineation of the milking limits on Plate IV, facing p. 84, for the U.S.S.R.

[6] Adametz, *op. cit.* [see Gen. Refs.]; ref. on pp. 80–85.

[7] E. Douglas van Buren: Fauna and Flora of Ancient Mesopotamia as Represented in Art, *Analecta Orientalia*, Vol. 18, 1939; ref. on p. 70.

[8] Max Hilzheimer, *op. cit.* [see Gen. Refs. under Brehm]; ref. on pp. 48–57.

[9] Bengt Lundholm: Abstammung und Domestikation des Hauspferdes, *Zoologiska bidrag från Uppsala*, Vol. 27, Uppsala, 1947.

[10] Piggott, *op. cit.*, pp. 121, 126, 157–158.

[11] J. Iversen: Land Occupation in Denmark's Stone Age, *Danmarks Geol. Undersøgelse*, Ser. 2, No. 66, Copenhagen, 1941.

[12] Grahame Clark, *op. cit.*

Supplements

AGE AND AREA OF AMERICAN CULTIVATED PLANTS

CULTURAL FACTORS IN PLANT DOMESTICATION
IN THE NEW WORLD

MAIZE INTO EUROPE

Age and Area of American Cultivated Plants

Their Tropical Origin

The plants and animals domesticated in the New World originated almost in their entirety within tropical latitudes, some in tropical lowlands, a number in temperate altitudes, and others in cold highlands, but well within the limits of the two tropic circles. What was added beyond in higher latitudes was minor, marginal in location and utility, and apparently late; it included no animals; none of the plants became major crops, nor were any of them adopted far from their place of origin.

North of Mexico there were added to cultivation several plums and two grapes — fruits sufficiently ameliorated by Indian planting and selection to have yielded cultivated forms. The tuberous sunflower is native to the Mississippi Valley and was grown in Indian gardens on the East Coast; once planted it needs hardly any care and multiplies readily year after year. The plums and grapes are at home in the open, deciduous Eastern Woodlands; they received attention in historical time especially at the hands of Southeastern tribes such as the Muskhogean ones, who were pretty good farmers and lived in permanent "towns" with "gardens." To an an-

This article was originally published in *Actas del XXXIII Congreso Internacional de Americanistas* (San José, Costa Rica, 1959), Vol. I, pp. 215-229.

cient seed complex brought out of Mexico by people unknown, there were added here to cultivation some fruits and
a tuber as minor extensions of an introduced complex. It
cannot be claimed that the lands to the north of the Tropics
lacked plants or animals suitable for cultivation and domestication. We have in the United States a flora rich in edible
seeds, fruits, and nuts; we have diverse tubers and bulbs that
were dug for food; a number of native plant species are at
present the object of successful selection. No animal was domesticated in the North, though kinds attractive to man and
amenable to breeding by him are probably more numerous
than in the South. For instance, the southern Mexico turkey, not any of the northern species, became the domestic
animal. The methods and the plants of agriculture came
from the South long ago; the North added a few minor elab-
orations.

Extratropical South America was less deeply penetrated
by agriculture than was North America, its principal plants
again having been carried in from tropical latitudes. The
farthest extension was in Chile, where two plants were added
to and altered by cultivation, a grass (*Bromus mango*) and a
tarweed for its oily seeds (*Madia sativa*). Both colonize freely
on fallow or poorly cultivated fields and may be considered
as having entered tilled land as weeds towards the boreal
limits of potatoes, beans, quinoa, and maize. In seasons in
which these staples did poorly, mango and madia provided
an alternate harvest. First tolerated and increased under cultivation of the standard crops, these came to be adopted as
crop insurance and became to some extent changed from
their wild state.

The development of New World agriculture took place
in our low latitudes, where man fashioned to his uses a great

diversity of plants, further largely diversified by breeding. These constitute as varied and genial a solution of producing food and other prime materials as was achieved anywhere in the world. In time some of these cultigens were carried into far parts of North and South America, extending the aboriginal limits of agriculture nearly to the climatic limits of modern farming. Still later they contributed greatly, both in New and Old World, foods and fiber plants that made possible the modern world.

The primordial area of domestication was greatly less than that of the Tropics. All wet lands and also the year round rainy climates are out of consideration. In contrast to the Old World we lack hydrophytic cultigens; the New World crop plants are not suited to land that becomes water logged or is more than briefly flooded. Our native cultivators hardly knew anything of artificial land drainage. Where agricultural settlement entered poorly drained areas it sought out spots of adequate natural drainage, such as natural levees, or it improved soil aeration by heaping earth into mounds, as in flood plain cultivation of manioc and maize. The Mexican chinampas may be cited as a special device to aerate the soil. The sites eligible to primitive cultivation were selected for good drainage and loose soil — river banks and levees, small valleys of sufficient gradients, piedmont slopes, ridge crests, and even steep hill and mountain flanks of sufficient depth of soil. Relief as such was no deterrent to primitive tillage, but lack of relief was, the more so the greater the rainfall. The more rain and flooding the less were lowland plains of valley or coast amenable to agricultural occupation. Uplands in rain forest were colonized in the course of time where the soil was sufficient and friable, but the plants cultivated are not natives of the rain forest. At the other extreme, permanently arid lands became accessible to cultivators only after skills in spreading water were known, nor are the plants grown there native to arid climates.

The growth habits show to some degree a common climatic background. They fit into the rainfall regimen of the outer Tropics (sometimes called Savanna climates), with rainy season at the time of overhead sun, dry season at the low positions of the sun. On the equatorial side such seasonal contrast may merge into all-year round moistness, on the polar side into permanent aridity. The plants in question perhaps can be assigned, each to its niche, somewhere within the range of Savanna climates or to their mesothermal equivalent at higher elevations. The storage of starch in fleshy underground stems is an adaptation by perennial plants to alternation of dry and wet season. Such make use of the rainy season for growth, including the setting of tubers and the like, and, their growth accomplished, are ready for the following dry season, indifferent to its length and severity. The annuals mature after the rains stop. Each, we may say, has built into itself its own adaptation to a particular rhythm and amplitude of wet and dry season. Arrowroot (*Maranta*) and allouia (*Calathea*) tolerate a lot of dryness; yuca (*Manihot*) has markedly strong drought resistance. On the other hand the sweet potato (*Ipomoea batatas*) needs abundant moisture for several months and the basic maize is strikingly mesophytic, as shown by its shallow root system, large growth, and free transpiration from large leaf surfaces.

The Agricultural Hearth North of the Equatorial Area

The southern side of the American tropics is not advantageously located to have witnessed the beginnings of agriculture. Ethnologically and archeologically it is cultural hinterland, primitive, or late of penetration by advanced cultures. Nor does it have the appropriate flora ancestral to our domesticated plants, nor yet the properly attractive physical geography. The indicated location for a major agricultural hearth is on the mainland northern side of our tropics, about the Caribbean, southward into Ecuador, and northward into Mexico.

Here we meet with 1) an extraordinarily diversified terrain, due largely to the virgation of the Andean ranges and basins against the Caribbean Sea and to numerous volcanic cones and flows, 2) soils derived from diverse parent materials, including deep, friable, and fertile soils of volcanic origin, 3) marked differences in climate within short distances, due to relief and exposure, 4) great diversity of higher plant forms, including the near relatives of almost all the cultivated and domesticated kinds, 5) streams and lakes in number, rich in aquatic and riparian animal life. 6) The high physical and biotic diversity provided a diversity of habitats for man, each of restricted extent, favoring cultural provincialism but not to the extent of being adversely isolative. 7) In the larger geographic context the area was the great corridor and crossroads of the New World. 8) In this connection we should also note that the land leads northward by easy approach to the Mexican highlands and southward into the Andes. By its geologic structure Colombia provides good agricultural experiment stations from tropical coasts to high páramos. Also the structural basins of Magdalena and Cauca are ramps leading gradually upward and southward to the Andean altiplano. These interior passageways, rather than the external flanks of the Andes with their barrier zones of cloud and rain forest and of desert southward, were the avenues by which agriculture, if it spread from lower lands, could most readily establish itself in the cold interior of the Andes.

The hearth indicated provided also, by means of fishing and hunting, aquatic and riparian, the possibility of living in sedentary communities before agriculture was known. Such precondition I hold necessary. The initiators of domestication required a comfortable and dependable margin above mere survival, permanent homes, and a living in communities in which they could share observations and have the leisure to begin the long range experimentation that led to domestication. The business of plant growing and selection did not proceed from "prelogical minds" by hocus-pocus or chance. It required ease, continuity, and peace. It was carried out by acutely observing individuals, primitive systematists and geneticists we may assert, who taught others to identify and select, by lore and skill handed from generation to generation. The plants fashioned by man are artifacts of skilled craftsmen; plant breeders anywhere are still few and exceptional individuals. I have difficulty in visualizing the spontaneous and independent origins of agricultural living and arts by reaching an unelucidated "stage" or "level" of cultural advance, or by assuming that people turned to producing food because they were getting hungrier. Distressed folk were least likely to have the capital reserves for investment in deferred returns. Such progress I should look for as originating in a most favored area, with a society amenable to new ways and recognizing original talent in its individuals. Were such congenial physical and cultural situations present as well anywhere else in the New World?

Vegetative Planting

To the English colonists of North America Indian agriculture meant Indian corn, Indian beans, and squash for which they borrowed the Indian name; to the Portuguese in South America mandioca (yuca in Spanish) was the Indian staple. Seed agriculture in the North; roots grown from cuttings in the South. Where the two systems meet anthropologists identify the Mesoamerican as against Circumcaribbean culture. Did each system arise independently, or is one derivative from the other? Which the elder? Why the difference? What effects where they have been in contact? These are questions which we must ask and to which we may bring pieces of evidence, if not complete answers. If seeking understanding of events and processes, using data of whatever kind appear related on reasonable examination, is speculation, it is only by such circumstantial evidences that the events and their order may be reconstructed.

The vegetative reproduction that dominated South American agriculture has a common distinctive pattern: 1) Reproduction is asexual, that is the new plant is grown from a piece of another plant, not from its seed. A tuber or piece thereof, a division of the root stock, a shoot, or a cutting of stem is planted, to grow into a complete plant. In its beginnings this is the most primitive means of propagation: Digging tubers gave an incomplete harvest; what was missed set a new crop in the disturbed ground, to be dug in another year. Such digging plots tended to become perennially productive. Another instance is the reproduction of waste parts of plants that were dropped on village refuse heaps. Transition from collecting to cultivation was thus facilitated. For each plant that became the object of continued cultivation a standard or conventional method of plant division seems to have become established. The plants thus taken under cultivation are perennials; their use by man rarely was for their seeds.

2) With the change from digging to planting, perhaps from

digging stick to planting stick, the way was opened for deliberate and individual selection. The prepared planting ground, or conuco, became the spot into which pieces of preferred individual plants were set. Where the planter recognized that the progeny was like the parent he began to select and reject and amelioration of the planting stock was under way. The multiplication of the desired plant was further advanced by the discovery, as in yuca and batata, that numerous stem cuttings could be taken to increase the progeny of a single parent. The whole road of domestication here rests on individual selection. After the initial selection from wild populations, further variation was provided by occasional (root) bud sports and by attractively variant accidental seed progeny that was saved for vegetative reproduction. Peasant cultivators in the Island of Haiti where yuca often still produces viable seeds, are well aware that the seed progeny is highly variable; such are now usually destroyed, since these are less likely to produce desirable plants. In early days however such variants provided an important means of improvement. By individual plant selection of the more desirable forms, long continued in various environments, a large diversity of races was developed.

3) Because the planter was always concerned with vegetative reproduction the plants that were thus fashioned in many cases lost the ability to reproduce themselves by seed. The forms of such sterility are various and in part still unstudied. Sterile plants became wholly dependent on the care of man for their survival. Where Europeans rudely overran native cultures many such forms were lost by flight or death of the natives, by the abandonment of conucos, or were rooted out by the introduced pigs. A generation after the beginning of Spanish occupation of Haiti Oviedo noted with

regret that a number of the best kinds of batatas, for which he wrote down the native names, had become extinct.

4) The attention to food production was mainly directed to underground parts, fleshy roots and tubers, to be harvested by digging. Unlike the Old World tropics (*Alocasia,* sugar cane, *Musa ensete*) no plants were developed for the food value of their stems. A few plants became vegetative cultigens for the fruits they yielded, with various resultant degrees and forms of sterility. Such are the peach palm or pejibae (*Bactris utilis*), the better races of which are reproduced by cuttings, the pepino (*Solanum muricatum*) resembling in quality both cucumber and melon, and the pineapple (*Ananas*), which may have had early attention as a fiber plant.

The case of the peanut (*Arachis*), called groundnut by the English, is peculiar. It is grown for its seeds and is planted from seed, but since it buries its pods in the ground and thus simulates a root crop and is harvested by digging or pulling the whole plant out of the ground, we have a functional resemblance to root culture. Does this help to explain why out of a host of herbaceous and suffrutescent species of Leguminosae in South America it stands nearly alone as product of cultivation?

5) The plants vegetatively domesticated contribute starch and sugar to the diet, but very little protein, fats, or oils. It seems obvious that there was no interest in, or need of a balanced vegetable diet. The plants were developed to increase the supply of carbohydrates and they did so effectively. The lack of attention to seed production means that no need was felt to increase the availability of proteins and fats. In contrast to the Old World tropics the great cultural possibilities of palms in the New World remained largely unstudied by

Europeans; one of the few exceptions, pejibae, was selected for increase of the starchy flesh surrounding the seed and toward the elimination of endosperm.

The meaning of such one-sided agriculture is clear: protein and fats were provided from animal sources. The inferred hearth area, the mainland adjacent to the Caribbean, was richly thus stocked, especially along both fresh and salt water. Fish, shell-fish and turtles abounded. Flocks of migrant water fowl from the north come here in winter. The sea cow or manati, feeding in the lower stream courses, was once the great game animal. Various hystricomorphs, partly of aquatic habits, provided excellent meat in quantity. Tapirs, and in part peccary and deer, fed along the side of streams. Animal food, and thereby protein and fat, was in surplus supply; the need was for more carbohydrates and planting was limited in attention to supplying such need. This specialized agriculture points emphatically to an origin among fishing and hunting people living along streams and lakes, in permanent communities.

6) Unlike seed agriculture, hardly any special procedures are required for harvest or storage. The roots remain in the ground and are dug as needed; usually they keep better in the ground than in storage. Provision is day by day; the calendar may have a planting time when the rains begin but it lacks a season of harvest and attendant ceremonial.

7) The processing of food is simple; it merely needs to be cooked. Milling is unnecessary. The roots may be roasted at the edge of the fire or they can be wrapped in mud or in leaves and baked. Steam cooking in covered pits over a bed of coals is an ancient and excellent means of preparing a meal of roots, flesh and fish. The barbacoa is characteristic of this area; such a grill over a low fire serves as well for

cooking roots as for cooking and drying meat or fish. That pottery vessels were preceded by gourds is recorded in the preceramic agricultural sites of coastal Peru, one of the few areas where agriculture was not associated with the making of pottery. The Caribbean lands are the home of the domesticated calabash tree (*Crescentia cujete*), selected vegetatively to a variety of sizes and forms of calabashes, light and durable containers. Columbus noted them as used for bailing boats. They are still thus prized, as well as to carry water, for fermenting drinks, and to some extent for cooking.

In marginal areas a few crops were less simply prepared: In the Andes leaching and the complicated chuño process were added and in eastern South America the elaborate procedures of preparing bitter manioc.

The Diversity of Vegetatively Produced Starch Foods

Since they were concerned with getting more carbohydrate food the primitive fishermen collectors of the Tropics may well have exploited every edible root. Many of these took root in village refuse heaps, and the best were transplanted into conucos when such were begun. But why have so many been kept in cultivation, changed so greatly from their original form, and diversified into so large a number of races? It is reasonable to think that at the dawn of agriculture many things were planted, but why have so many been continued to the present merely to supply the same kind of starch food? That has been and is really their one use. Some are used a little for greens. None serves for fibre or other domestic or personal ends.

The consumer takes in calories and that is about the size of it; he may be expected to discriminate against the less nourishing kinds and the less productive ones and in time thus to have dropped their cultivation. It is hardly reasonable that the same people should have kept up the breeding of a lot of different plants serving quite the same purpose and requiring the same attention at the same time. With one satisfactory or promising starch source available the long and tedious effort to ameliorate another wild plant to serve the same needs though inferior in yield would not have been continued, yet the characteristic situation today is that several such, economically more and less rewarding, are cultivated in the same locality and in the same ground.

Aboriginal cultivation by vegetative reproduction dominated one great, continuous New World area and only that area. It looks very much as though the idea was spread by contagion from one community to another culturally receptive one. (That this was not a matter of presence or absence of suitable plants will be considered later.) Useful plants were dug or grew on refuse heaps in many places over the world without giving rise to agriculture and plant breeding. The decisive first step, followed by the next ones necessary to create an enduring agricultural system, perhaps was taken once and in one restricted area. We shall hardly expect to locate place, time, or plants of earliest domestication since we cannot say that higher age and larger area agree, nor even that the diversification of a cultigen is an expression of its age.

The most apparent reason for the diversity of cultivated starch plants in tropical America is that they fitted into different climatic conditions. Breeding in time has blurred such environmental advantage or disadvantage, though much less on the whole than in seed cultigens. Much needs to be learned about the climatic range of each species and its component forms, but we can recognize that arrowroot (*Maranta*) and allouia (*Calathea*) are tierra caliente plants indifferent to drought, whereas yampee (*Dioscorea trifida*) and pejibae (*Bactris*), also of the hot lowlands, are exacting of moisture. The marked climatic contrasts within short distances support the hypothesis of substitutive domestications. Thus may the agricultural way of life have moved upslope from tierra caliente, if that was its earlier home, through the tierra templada and into the tierra fría, finding in each amenable and rewarding plants for cultivation. Racacha (*Arracacia*) and llacón (*Polymnia*) I know only from temperate lands in northwestern South America. Oca (*Oxalis*), ulluco (*Ullucus*), and ysaño (*Tropaeolum*) are restricted to Andean highlands. *Canna edulis* and yautia or malanga (*Xanthosoma*) are grown here and there in both hot and temperate country.

Locally racacha, yautia, and pejibae still are staples. Mainly the plants named are being cultivated less and less. Originally they may have enjoyed environmental superiority in their home locality, but they are held in cultivation to the present mainly by the persistence of cultural tradition; other plants have been developed that grow as well and yield more, on the same sort of land, with the same kind of labor used on the same calendar. Their persistence suggests that they were grown before the economically superior yuca, potatoes, and sweet potatoes were available.

In the course of time the ascendancy of yuca (manioc) in the low country and of potato in the highlands became so marked that Clark Wissler could with some justice divide South America into two agricultural regions identified by these plants. Manioc types were developed that did well in tierra templada and others that succeeded under rain forest cultivation. The range of variation of this cultigen is not as yet well studied. Sweet forms extend throughout the range of

[125]

cultivation of manioc; the bitter ones (with their special techniques of processing) are Atlantic and did not enter Central America or western South America.

What happened to the potato at the hands of man is one of the better known chapters of domestication. Wild potatoes, with edible tubers, range in a very large number of species from Colorado to southern Chile and Brazil. Within this range they are unrecorded only in tierra caliente and deserts, but are numerous in temperate as well as cold climes. Only a few have entered into forming the great complex of cultivated potatoes, diploid and polyploid. One hearth is in Colombia and Ecuador, the other in southern Peru and adjacent Bolivia, with cultivated forms occurring from the lower parts of tierra templada to the cold limits of agriculture. (Knowledge of their phylogeny has been advanced especially by the work of J. G. Hawkes in the Imperial Bureau of Plant Breeding and Genetics, Cambridge). Most of the cultivated potatoes set fertile seeds; accidental hybrid offspring, in part involving one wild parent, has maintained variation at a high level. Selection in cultivation has been by tubers so that the possibilities of multiplying and increasing clones are almost unlimited. Cultivated potatoes were spread throughout the Andes from Venezuela to Chile to the upper climatic limits of agriculture. They were also taken from the Bolivian highlands to extratropical lowland Chile as far as the polar limit of aboriginal agriculture in Chile.

The Limits of Vegetative Planting

In South America the system of vegetative reproduction was extended to the limits of agriculture, both as to latitude and altitude. With certain exceptions, such as the arid west coast, it continued to be the dominant system. Northward it occupied the West Indies and the Caribbean side of Central America, but did not enter the Southeastern United States at all and got to Mexico in a minor way for a short distance and with only a few plants. Of these the sweet potato found largest acceptance in Mexico, but was nowhere a major crop and, by its Nahua name, appears to have been of late introduction. It seems not to have reached the northern limit of high native culture even in the tropical lowlands, excellently suited to it. Spaniards took it into northern Mexico and Englishmen into the United States; the Indians knew it not. This failure to spread in North America is in striking contrast to its dissemination across the Pacific into high latitudes. The peanut had a similar story; the form in native Mexican cultivation resembles the type in Peruvian archeology. The pineapple was cultivated somewhat in the hot country as far north as the Tepic area. The slight attention given to yuca is somewhat surprising, considering how well it grows and yields; it too got a descriptive name, huaucamote, "the woody plant with edible roots." None of these plants approached any climatic or other physical limit; they petered out in non-receptive cultures.

This assertion that northward (the Mesoamerica of anthropology) the cultures were non-receptive to the system of agriculture by vegetative reproduction is based on two considerations. The first is the mentioned fact of the fading out of such cultigens northward for no physical reason. The second is that no native plants, useful to man and suited to such reproduction were developed in the North. I should hesitate to say that such were less available or that they remained unappreciated. An edible tuberous Manihot (*M. carthaginensis?*) grows on the west coast into southern Arizona and is collected. Camotes del cerro, one of which is a Euphorb

(*Dalembertia*), are common and appreciated boiled tubers, sold in markets and on streets of interior Mexico. The Mexican highlands have a number of species of wild potatoes of some current interest to potato breeders. These grow as volunteers in the milpas, especially on the slopes of the Mexican volcanoes. They are dug and used, even sold to some extent in markets. They are small, but of good taste, and quite prolific. Some remain in the ground and restock the milpa for the next year. The cultivators, Indians who retain much of their culture, appreciate them and give them some protection, but they do not plant them and of course practice no selection. The orientation northward is that of seed planting and away from root or stem cuttings. To the north we enter a differently minded world in agricultural procedures.

Tobacco and Alcohol

The plants taken farthest north from South America were three seed-produced, nonedible cultigens, a cotton, a tobacco, and the Lagenaria gourd. The bottle gourd is common in archeologic sites well up into the United States. It may perhaps have been introduced northward about as far as it would grow. Cotton of the western American lineage (*G. hirsutum* complex) became the textile fiber of the Mexican lowlands, cotton cloth (mantas) being a chief tribute item out of the hot country to the Aztec state. It was also established at intermediate elevations in the highlands of Mexico and seems to have been taken to the American Southwest in early Christian times (Hohokam). It never reached the Mississippi Valley or southeastern United States.

Of the two cultivated tobaccos *Nicotiana tabacum* remained closely associated with the vegetative planters; if it got into Mexico before the Spaniards, it did so only slightly, in the lowlands. The other, *N. rustica,* became second only to maize in its agricultural dispersal. That it was the more widely accepted may be attributed in part to its lesser need of attention but also to its much higher nicotine content. Its original home is placed in the highland border of Peru and Ecuador. It was the great tobacco of Mexico, picietl, and is known to us as Aztec tobacco. It was generally grown by the Indians of our Eastern Woodlands as far as the lower St. Lawrence Valley. Man's interest centered in its alkaloid, nicotine, of all narcostimulants the one of widest appeal for ritual use. In its original home *N. rustica* was taken by drink; it was thence spread into areas where narcotics were used by chewing and as snuff, and still farther, as in North America, to be smoked in pipes. The physiologic effect having been recognized, the plant was adopted into different, probably preexistent ceremonial practices, passing from culture to culture.

Tropical American planters concerned themselves, as did men in few other parts of the world, with plant poisons, with piscicides and poisoned projectiles, with stimulants and narcotics, with medication by effective drugs as well as by magic. Valid observational taxonomy and experimental biochemistry were joined in appropriating plant resources in rather sophisticated ways. The tropical growers of food were also skilled manipulators of potent drugs and poisons and some of these are cultigens. Thus the Solanaceae (Nightshade Family) were pretty fully exploited in domestication; Potatoes for food and dye, pepino, naranjilla (Solanum quitoense), Cyphomandra, Physalis as fruits and vegetables, Capsicum as seasoning and medicine, and Nicotiana and Datura as drugs.

Alcoholic beverages were common, in so far as I know, to

all the vegetative planting folk. Drinking was ceremonially restricted, especially to feasts, and varied as to moderation or excess in different parts. Spanish chroniclers thought some of the tribes of the Cauca basin of western Colombia given to extreme drunkenness. Sweet fruit and palm sap were fermented but the main employment was of starch food plants, the fermentation aided by mastication in South America. Only farmers brewed. Northward alcoholic beverages were common to all the farming peoples of Mexico but were not used by the Pueblo people of the Southwest nor by the farming tribes of the interior and eastern United States. Roughly the boundary between Mexico and the United States was the northern limit of alcoholic beverages. The area in which alcoholic drinking was established is one and continuous. To the north it included only the Mesoamerican culture, into which it is concluded that it was introduced from the South, but beyond which the farming tribes, though growing the same complex of crops, did not adopt the practice.

The Seed Farmers

The northern hearth of plant domestication, where the process was done by seeds and therefore by sexual selection, lies in southern Mexico and northern Central America. The wild relatives of the cultivated plants grow here; the cultivated forms are here in greatest diversity. Consensus favors this area and I know no reason to disagree. The basic complex is simple, maize, beans and squash, with grain amaranth as a relic, still widely occurring in small cultivation. For the hearth area chile (*Capsicum*), chia (*Salvia hispanica*), and "tomate" (*Physalis ixocarpa* as the term tomato is restricted in Mexican use) are included. The classical form of milpa planting is maize, beans, squash set into the same mound or hole, the beans climbing up the corn stalks, the squash spreading over the ground, the three together forming effective utilization of sunlight and rain and giving protection against rain wash. The milpa system resembles that of the conuco in these important particulars: 1) The seeds are set by hand into the exact spot where they are to grow; they are not sown broadcast or in rows. 2) A number of different plants are grown together in the same ground. 3) Where soil permits, the planting is in mounded earth, "hilling" in the terms of the American farmer. 4) Selection is practiced by saving seed from desirable individual plants, as by ear of corn, vine or pods of beans, or a particular squash that is set aside to be used for seed. It is still a planting system.

The food orientation of this system is however very different from that of the vegetative planters. The object here is dietary balance, a proper and adequate supply of protein and fat, as well as carbohydrates. This adequacy was achieved here by plant foods as well and as economically as anywhere in the world. The need of animal food is small, the implication that, when agriculture began here it began on the basis, not of one kind of supplementary food as was the case in the South, but of a complete diet, high in protein content. This interest in protein was marked in the origins of domestication. The seeds of squashes are still as important a food as is their flesh. Tzilacayote (*Cucurbita ficifolia*), an ancient domesticate, is of little account for its flesh except in making fermented drink (or now as stock feed), but its large, numerous, and tasty seeds are appreciated. There still are races of *C. moschata* that are grown only for their oily, nutty seeds. The development of squashes for starchy and sweet flesh came later, as did that of the large mealy beans, and of floury maize.

The dietary bias in domestication was initially toward protein and fat, with later breeding to increase carbohydrate yield.

(It may be more than a coincidence that the domestic bird of this agriculture is the turkey, inhabitant of temperate oak and pine woodlands, whereas a tropical river duck, the, muscovy, was taken into the households of the root planters.)

There is an air of temperate Mexican and Guatemalan uplands about these cultivated seed plants, as though they had moved from open woodland into clearings, which is exactly what may well have happened. The cultivated beans are all climbers, the Indian runner (*P. multiflorus*) being a vine of astonishing growth. Of the Cucurbits a single plant of chayote (*Sechium edule*) will provide a bower (ramada) for the open air living of a household. Is this plant, useful alike for its fruits and starchy roots (as is the runner bean) a link between vegetative and seed planting ways? Wild cucurbits are common in open spaces such as old fields, as are amaranths where pigs and cattle do not destroy them. The wild kin of the plants in question are vigorous colonizers of clearings and their margins. The surmise may be kept in mind that the first seed cultivators were inland dwellers in temperate lands, of limited resource for fishing and waterside hunting. As they turned to planting, their attention shifted from roots to the seeds of cucurbits, beans and amaranths that came up as volunteers in clearing. I am not competent to comment on the origin of maize, but both Tripsacum and Euchlaena are weeds of fields.

The Spread of Mesoamerican Seed Plants

The variety of plants grown became reduced north of the line of volcanoes that stretches across Mexico. Only a few kinds reached eastern United States, and they of course came from Mexico. An attractive task for archeology is the exploration of rock shelters for the cultivated plant remains left by early occupants, such as those already recovered in Tamaulipas, New Mexico, and the Ozarks, in the present state of our knowledge the most ancient on record.

Southward maize, beans and squashes filtered throughout the agricultural parts of South America, as associates of root crops. Maize rarely became the staple crop in South America. It was planted, especially across northern South America, in tropical flint varieties, for the making of beer, and was boiled or roasted as immature ears (choclo of the Andes). Beans and squashes mostly were minor additions to conuco planting. However, on the arid west coast and beyond into the latitudes of Chile, they became dominant crops; here the lima bean (pallar) acquires its greatest importance. Junius Bird's discovery of the preceramic agriculture of the arid west coast brought as one of its greatest surprises the knowledge that the little esteemed tzilacayote (*Cucurbita ficifolia*) was grown there before maize or true beans were introduced. Also, at this early time *Cucurbia moschata* was beginning to be planted in coastal Peru. Farther south *C. moschata* later apparently gave rise to the only South American squash, *C. maxima,* by crossing with some wild Cucurbita. (The knowledge of Cucurbita domesticates is due mainly to the work of Dr. Thomas Whitaker of the U.S. Department of Agriculture at La Jolla, California).

New World agriculture, it is here proposed, had its beginnings in tropical lowlands by vegetative reproduction and selection of starch food plants. It made the ascent to high altitudes in the Andes by applying the same art and attention to other tuberous plants. At the north in Central America, it changed to seed growing that satisfied nearly the whole range of dietary needs. These seed plants in turn found entry into South America root planting, probably as population increased and animal sources of food became inadequate or depleted. Aboriginal agriculture occupied one continuous area in the New World, beyond which lie lands equally attractive as to climate, fertility, and plants, such as western Cuba, parts of the western United States such as California, and the central Argentine. Multiple independent invention of agriculture is therefore less acceptable than the spread of an art and its artifacts from a common hearth in low latitudes with derivative changes, substitutions, and exchanges over a long time and large distances.

Cultural Factors in Plant Domestication in the New World

The New World was occupied by way of the Far North by colonists who depended on the use of fire and the making of pointed shafts. Both were principal skills in securing food, both plant and animal. All historically known natives of the New World have practiced setting fire to vegetation as an aid to collecting and hunting and those who practiced tillage made use of fire in preparing the ground for planting. The longer the presence of primitive man, the greater has been the impress of fire on plant reproduction. Only the continually wet and the most arid lands have retained a plant cover unmodified by fire. Plants that grow in the sun have been given advantage over those in shade, herbaceous over woody ones, and so have those that reproduce by underground stems and shoots. To varying degree our vegetation is an artificial assemblage of ancient origins.

The outer tropical latitudes have a period of summer rains followed by a rainless season when the ground dries out to depth, in annual alternation of mesophytic and xerophytic condition. Adaptive modifications of plants to a dry period are many and marked, including fleshy roots. Also, the

This paper was originally presented at a symposium entitled "The Origin and Evolution of Cultivated Plants" held during the Tenth International Botanical Congress, 1964, and published in *Euphytica*, Vol. 14, 1965, pp. 301–306.

cumulative effects of burning have accentuated and extended such vegetation of xeric forms. The term *savanna* passed into European usage from the Indians of Haiti and means tropical grasslands with or without scattered trees or clumps of shrubs, largely, I think, formed by burning. The original meaning has been expanded in academic usage to tropical lands marked by annual cycle of dry and rainy seasons, whatever the plant cover.

It is in these "savanna" climates, on the boreal side of the equatorial rain forests, that the steps leading to plant cultivation in the New World probably are to be sought. The entry of man had been out of the north, moving from high latitudes gradually into the tropics. The fauna to the south continued to be largely familiar; the flora mainly became different. A new economic botany needed to be learned for a large diversity of plants. In the high country of Middle America familiar seeds, acorns, and nuts still were available for harvest in the fall season. From Texas and Arizona south through Mexico the summer brought large harvest of cactus fruits of many kinds, the seasonal staple first described in the wanderings of Cabeza de Vaca. In the passage of this dry belt, that extends from coast to coast on both sides of the International Boundary, new learning was secured of food to be had from roots and stems. Here men learned to roast the scapes and the turgid buds of diverse agavaceous plants, of common record in the remains of early rock shelters from Arizona and Baja California into the Mexican Meseta. In large measure, this source of food was available through much of the year or continuously. In Central America starch was extracted from the trunks of *Acrocomia* palms. Most of all, the digging stick was used to discover large food resources at all seasons in fleshy roots, tubers, bulbs. Starch stored in underground parts

was found in many kinds of plants, Aroids, Dioscoreas, *Canna,*
Maranta, Euphorbs, Solanums, *Ipomoea,* Cucurbits, Leguminosae, Compositae. Some are herbaceous, others suffruti-
cose, and some are shrubs. *Manihot carthaginensis,* which has
good, sweet tubers, forms a stout shrub native to tierra
caliente from the Gulf of California south to northern South
America. Cooked wild tubers are still sold in local markets,
in Mexico called *camotes del cerro.* The migration of man
down the narrowing corridor of Mexico and Central America
and on to the southern side of the Caribbean Sea was an exer-
cise in the nutritive potentials of the carbohydrates stored in
vegetative parts.

Digging roots had several advantages over seed collecting.
The roots could be dug as needed at any time of year. No
provision for storage was needed. Seeds set poorly in an adverse season whereas the supply of roots is little affected thus.
Most significantly, digging is in effect involuntary cultivation.
It loosens the soil, giving better aeration and more room for
new tubers to grow. Harvest by digging stick or spade is incomplete, pieces of the root stock being missed or rejected.
These in turn become new plants, as any gardener knows to
his sorrow who has had to do with weeds that reproduce
vegetatively. Repeated digging of a patch thus is a means to
increase the number of such plants. Continued use tended to
maintain, even to increase the productivity of such digging
grounds. Various parts of the Mexican highlands may be cited
in illustration, where there are wild potatoes with small
but tasty tubers that are gathered and marketed. These are
now most commonly found growing in milpas of maize and
of other cultivated annuals. They are native species which
Professor Hawkes has studied and shown not to be derived
from or to have been made into the cultigen potatoes. They

are often found where potato growing is unknown and are not planted nor are they the object of cultivation, but are relicts or volunteers in the milpas and benefit from the tillage of the ground for maize. A side harvest of the little potatoes takes place which leaves enough of them in the ground to restock the milpa year after year. In some places the survival of these wild potatoes perhaps has depended on having been present in milpas.

Digging may thus be indicated as the first step towards plant domestication. In the case of the Mexican potatoes it has not led to a second step. Primitive man all over the world may have dug food plants wherever he could and for a very long time without becoming thereby a cultivator or plant breeder. The diversity and abundance of plants thus attractive and native to many parts of Middle America continued for a time, perhaps for a long time, to give adequate food supply from such digging plots, enlarged by fire to give more cleared land, fire being the immemorial adjunct to increased food production, plant and animal.

The next step is not to be construed as a stage entered on by reaching a certain level of cultural development. Centers of plant domestication about the world are few and as we learn more such independent centers become still fewer. The immediate concern is with plants that were chosen for vegetative reproduction and selection. The hypothesis may be suggested that in the New World this idea arose in a single region, namely on the Tierra Firme side of the Caribbean.

A singular mode of production took shape here, known as the *conuco*. The name is taken from the island of Haiti, as are the names of so many of the plants grown. It was there that Europeans first came to know this form of tillage. As the ground is dug it is heaped into mounds as high as is convenient. Such piling up of earth provides aeration of soil on wettish lands, protects against sheetwash on slopes, and provides loose ground for the fleshy roots. The mounds are laborious to make but convenient to maintain. Conucos are not features of shifting cultivation. Into these mounds pieces of the plants to be propagated are inserted, segments of stems in the case of manioc, young shoots of sweetpotato vines, the leafcrown of pineapple, a rhizome of arrowroot, in some cases an above ground part, in others an underground one. The intention is to reproduce the plant desired by taking a piece of it which will grow into another identical plant. Selection is by individual plant. By continuing vegetative reproduction some kinds have lost, or for the most part have lost, the capacity of sexual reproduction. Inserting pieces of plants into such mounds made it convenient and desirable to grow different plants in the same mound.

The interest of this form of cultivation is not to diversify food but to provide starch abundantly and continuously, some of the plants also being used as greens. There is hardly any place in the complex for oil or protein yielding plants, the principal exception, the peanut, being only a tidbit. Fat and protein continued to be supplied from animal sources, mainly aquatic. The food economy was based on fishing in the inclusive sense and on root crops. Such was the provision of balanced diet all about the Caribbean at the coming of the Europeans and had been from remote times.

Fishing people are likely to be sedentary, as shown by the depth of ancient kitchen middens. The harvest of sea and stream about the Caribbean was attractive throughout the year. In these low latitudes the aquatic resources varied little with season. There was no dead season. At times there were additional resources. Migrant water birds overwintered, marine turtles frequented beaches in their season to lay eggs. Properly chosen sites for permanent habitation near water were also suited to cultivate root crops. The pristine model is a fishing village with soil suitable for conucos near by.

The south side of the Caribbean is indicated for the beginnings of vegetative cultivation. Whatever early peoples were moving south through the New World had to move by the Isthmus of Panama into South America. In the eastern part of the Isthmus they encountered a tropical rainforest, scant of resource but which could be bypassed by foraging along shore and stream. A short distance East beyond the Gulf of Urabá, the climate changes to alternation of dry and wet season and so continues nearly to the eastern end of the Caribbean mainland. In parts the coast is arid, with rain increasing inland. The watersides, salt and fresh, were attractive for animal food. The virgation of the several Andean chains against the Caribbean gives large diversity of terrain, climates, soils, and flora. The complex of vegetatively cultivated plants is best assigned to origin here. Wild kindred of manioc, sweet potato, yautía (*Xanthosoma*), arrowroot, peach palm (*Bactris/Guilielma*), and pineapple are all found in these parts, the derivation of the cultigen remaining undetermined. Contingent upon genetic support the hypothesis that the American hearth of vegetative domestication lay to the south of the Caribbean rests on its location as gateway and center of dispersal of cultures across South America, into the West Indies and Central America, on the presence of suitable parent plants, on the high elaboration of conuco cultivation, on the extraordinary fishing skills, and on the increasing archeologic evidence that man was present early and made large cultural advance here. In comparison, Brazil which has been cited for such origins is culturally marginal, late and backward.

The Spaniards were impressed by the economic competence of native life about the Caribbean, most so in the islands because these were first to be known and, being novel, were best described. They found a teeming population amply supported mainly by fishing, by cassava bread, the staff of life made from bitter manioc, and by sweet potatoes. The productivity of the conucos was far higher than that of any agriculture Europeans had known and was characterized by outstanding yields. Except for the Natural History of Oviedo and the comments of Columbus these observations have had little attention. Islands and Tierra Firme, as the south side of the Caribbean was called, were overrun so rapidly and brusquely that well populated and intensively cultivated regions went back to wilderness in a few years or became cattle ranches. Oviedo noted the complete dependence of such plants as sweet potatoes on human care and the extinction of a number of the best kinds by his time. Unlike Mexico and Peru there has been great loss of cultigens about the Caribbean. There are, however, many that have been maintained, such as starchy races of sweet potatoes, still largely unnoticed by science.

Fruit cultivation in the Caribbean is poorly documented. The Arawaks who inhabited the Greater Antilles were little interested. On Tierra Firme there was, however, horticulture and selection, particularly so in the western part. Here the papaya seems to belong. Its relation to wild Caricas, manner of selection, and aboriginal distribution are in need of study. The mamey (*Mammea*) is one of the more esteemed tropical fruits and was used for wine, which may account for the large stands of these trees that were reported from the Pacific side of Panama by the discoverers. Except for the Arawaks of the northern islands, the natives about the Caribbean indulged freely, and to the southwest did so greatly, in frequent and heavy alcoholic libations. Alcohol may not be neglected as a possible factor in plant domestication, the pineapple serving as an example. The non-alcoholic Arawaks of the islands, it is said by Las Casas, did not know that fruit until introduced by the Spaniards from the south. The island Caribs planted pineapples in fields and in Panamá there were large plantations of it for making wine. This may account for the long selection of this Bromeliad into the large and luscious fruit that the Spaniards esteemed above all others. Would native plant breeders have kept to the tedious task of selecting a small and acid fruited plant merely to have another fruit to eat in a country of diverse fruits? The pineapple might have been developed into a fibre plant but actually became a major source of wine, as potent as a fermented drink can be. Unlike the tropical fruit trees that bear for a short season a planting of pineapples yielded more or less continuously. Continuous supply of beverage was important, the knowledge of how to stop fermentation perhaps being mostly unknown. Wild or feral pineapples are of widespread occurence in the savannas of Colombia as they are in Brazil to which country the origin has been attributed for that reason. The pineapple was well and favorably known to the Spaniards from the second voyage of Columbus on and was an important item of Indian cultivation all about the southern side of the Caribbean, alcoholic beverage being the probable reason.

The only land route into South America that avoided wide expanse of rain forest led up the inter-Andean basins of

Colombia into the temperate and cool lands of the Andes, rich in deep volcanic soils. This open and inviting corridor is sometimes said to be the way by which people and agriculture entered the Andean highlands rather than by way of the rain drenched Montaña to the East or by the Pacific coast, with its rainiest of rain forests at the north, replaced southward by extreme desert. The Andean crop plants are also in the main roots. Sweet potatoes and racacha (*Arracacia*) are staples in temperate valleys, and both are of northern origin. In the highlands there is the famous diversity of cultigen potatoes along with the lesser tubers of ancient cultivation, *Ullucus tuberosus, Oxalis tuberosa* and *Tropaeolum tuberosum*. These three species are still important in highland Indian cultivation in Colombia as well as farther to the south. May not the planting of root crops have spread from the Colombian lowlands up the Andean ramp, tubers of temperate climate replacing those that did not thrive above the hot lowlands, and in turn giving way to others in the cold highlands? May not the same thing have happened to the potatoes, the multiple speciation of which Professor Hawkes has followed from Peru into Colombia and Venezuela, namely that the first domestication of potatoes took place in the North and was extended to the South, rather than begun in the Peruvian altiplano? *In fine* perhaps, that the whole idea of plant breeding by vegetative selection spread from one center throughout those parts of the southern continent where agriculture developed?

To the north, in upper Central America and Mexico, plant breeding had other purposes, procedures, and connections. Reproduction was by seed and the product was a seed crop. It was still a hilling and planting operation in which the desired number of seeds were hand-sown. Seeds of several kinds, as maize, beans, and squash, were and are planted together, and they are selected from a particular parent, as by ear of maize and pepo of Cucurbit. There was no broadcasting or mass selection and for the most part no segregation of plants in separate fields. In these respects the seed farming of the New World is akin to the root growing of the South.

A boundary of convenience and possible validity may be drawn between the root-minded and the seed-minded systems of tillage, running by way of the Straits of Florida, the Yucatan Channel, and the Gulf of Honduras across Central America to the Pacific about the Gulf of Nicoya. North and west of this demarcation root crops penetrated weakly if at all, sweet potatoes being an illustration of their failure to reach well suited more northerly areas. Within the northern area the tuberous sunflower is the lone addition of such a plant to cultivation, more a useful weed than an object of care.

The milpa of Mexico and Guatemala is the analogue of the conuco of the Caribbean. However, the seeds are grown to satisfy the major part of the dietary needs, animal food being of lesser importance. There are definite times of planting and of harvest. By paying attention to individual plant selection the size of seed has been much increased, as illustrated by comparison of Phaseoli cultivated in the New World with those in the Old World. This also provides the means to select for color and other qualities that attracted the attention of the plant breeders. The attention being directed to a certain time of harvest following the time of rains, heavily seeding annuals, such as *Amaranthus, Chenopodium,* and *Helianthus* were attractive. In some cases cultivated annuals were derived from wild perennials, such appearing to be the main origin of the cultigen *Cucurbitae* and *Phaseoli.*

To a large extent the ancestral forms may have been attractive weeds, as in the case of amaranths, chenopods, and sunflowers. Wild cucurbits occupy abandoned fields and wild beans clamber about the margins of milpas. *Tripsacum* which has entered into some kinds of maize is a competent volunteer in open spaces.

The origin of this seed complex raises questions. Is it independent of the root complex? Is it older or younger? Archeology has established an American age for it by the discoveries of R. McNeish almost as great as that of known agriculture in the Old World. A case can be made for the early care and improvement of the grain amaranths and chenopods and of the seed filled pepos of cucurbits, some of which are still grown for their seeds rather than for flesh. But what of the small-seeded wild beans, dehiscent, tedious to gather and prepare, and what of the miserable nubbins of the ancient maize? All these are eagerly harvested by birds and beasts and need to be watched over by those who grow them. Sedentary living is implied but on what did the people live during the long years when the seed plants developed into satisfactory producers of food?

If these seed domestications began in the south, that is in southern Mexico and northern Central America, and the native flora appears to be appropriate, an answer may be found. In such case sedentary tropical root planters could have made the clearings into which the ancestral seed plants moved as attractive volunteers. Such opportunity was at hand, especially in the temperate interiors, lands of oak and pine woods in Guatemala and southern Mexico. These boreal and altitudinal margins of root culture were floristically and ecologically suited for the development of seed cultivation.

The moot inference then is that the seed complex is derivative from root culture and originated in upper Central America.

Historical documentation in my *The Early Spanish Main,* Berkeley, 1966. Ethnobotanical references in my *Age and Area of American Cultivated Plants* in *33rd International Congress of Americanists,* San José, Costa Rica, 1959 (reprinted as the first supplement of this volume).

Maize Into Europe

Turkish Corn

A new natural science, uncommitted as to doctrine, followed quickly upon the Reformation and turned from classical authority to direct observation. In particular a plant
science took form that collected, described, and classified.
The new interest was in the identity of plants and where
they grew in contrast to the elder attention to their virtues
as simples according to Greek medical doctrine. Botany was
freed from traditional pharmacognosy. The break came first
in southern German lands that were strongly involved in the
religious dissent. Brunfels' *Herbarum Vivae Icones*, published in 1530 at Strasbourg, was the first of the new plant
descriptions that came to be known as the Great Herbals.
In these the recognition of all kinds of plants largely took
the place of medicinal use, and so previously unrecorded
plants unknown to Greek prescriptions were given attention.
Thus we find the first systematic accounts of maize, not as of
the earliest moment of its appearance in Europe, but as of
an emergent taxonomy.

A competent study of the growing knowledge of maize by
the herbalists of the sixteenth and seventeenth centuries has
been made by John Finan in his *Maize and the Great Herbals* (1950). He has the interesting finding that not until 1570

This article was originally published in *Akten des 34. Internationalen
Amerikanisten Kongresses* (Vienna, 1960), pp. 778–786.

was an American origin and introduction by way of Spain attributed to it in the herbals (by the Italian Matthioli, who had read Spanish chroniclers of the New World).

Hieronymus Bock, collecting in various parts of the Upper Rhine Valley, was first of the herbalists to describe maize. The work was first published in 1539, but was under way in 1531. He called it "the great *Welschkorn,* without doubt first brought to us by merchants from warm lands of fat soils . . . seed of three or four colors, some red, some brown, some yellow, and some pure white . . . in form like wild hazelnuts . . . yields a beautifully white meal." Perhaps, he thought, it should be called *frumentum asiaticum* from what he inferred to be its source. The designation *"Welsch"* suggested to southern Germans an immediate Italian source, *asiaticum* Asia Minor as farther derivation. This vagueness as to its introduction in the south of Germany also indicates that this took place prior to his own time.

The first use of the name *frumentum turcicum* (1536) was ascribed by DeCandolle to Jean Ruel(lius) of Paris, author of an old style translation of the materia medica of Dioscorides, with additional notes supplied by Ruel. Since he described a plant in part reminiscent of buckwheat, we may conclude only that he had heard of but had not seen Turkish corn, and hence that it was probably unknown in northern France.

The most famous of the herbals, that of Leonhart Fuchs, was first published in 1542, profusely and superbly illustrated by full folio page woodcuts that show in close detail the entire plants including roots. The costliness of the work delayed its publication, the formidable task of preparing it requiring from 1532 to 1538.[1] Fuchs was born in Bavaria and became professor (and repeatedly rector) at the University of Tübingen (1534 to his death). His observations appear to have been gathered mostly from parts of Suabia, then in active trade with Venice. The fine woodcut of maize bore the names *Turcicum Frumentum* and *Türckisch Korn,* he said, because it was first brought from Greece and Asia (both then under Turkish rule), adding that it was found passim in all gardens. Like Bock he named red-, purple-, yellow-, and white-seeded races and said it gave an excellent white meal.

Two illustrations earlier than the one by Fuchs are known. The first is in an Italian translation of Oviedo's first book, published in Venice in 1534 as *Sumario de la naturale historia* and probably drawn from maize growing in Venezia. The second may be a reduced copy of the former and appeared in the Seville edition of Oviedo in 1535. (I am indebted for the information to Francisco Aguilera of the Hispanic Foundation, Library of Congress.) At mid-century Ramusio in the first volume of his Voyages (*Navigationi e Viaggi*), also published at Venice, gave an exact reproduction of an ear of maize in its husk, showing plump, large, smooth kernels.

Finan has pointed out that Cordius (1561) was first to distinguish a kind with prop or brace roots and that l'Obel (1581) first illustrated this sort and distinguished it from a sort lacking prop roots, limiting the term Turkish corn to the older type.

The name Turkish corn has remained in use to the present, in Italy, for instance as *grano turco, sorgo turco,* and *soturco.* To dismiss such "Turkish corn" names as ignorant inventions seems prejudicial. There is no justification for saying that the new grain was attributed to Turkey because no one knew whence it came and Turkey was a casually convenient name for an alien and unknown source. A common argument used in support of such explanation is the English name for the Meleagrid fowl, which, however, in reality is not an accidental term. Nor is the inferred or explicit sequence sound that the New World was discovered by Spain and Portugal, that there had been no prior contact between the hemispheres, that maize could have been disseminated only by way of the Iberian Peninsula, and that this happened only in the decades following the discovery by Columbus.

We may therefore consider the alternative that the German herbalists were competent describers and did know what they were talking about. The South German towns were intermediaries in the great trade from North Italian ports, especially Venice, across the Alps to the Rhine and its tributaries; knowledge as well as goods flowed mainly out of the South into High Germany. Venice in particular was built on the Levantine trade, through which it rose to greatest wealth and power in the fifteenth century, at which time there were Venetian factories and colonies in number extending from the Adriatic to the easternmost Mediterranean. Venice had the closest contacts with the Ottoman Empire both before and after the fall of Byzantium. Nowhere in Europe were things "Turkish" so well known as in Venice. Nowhere north of the Alps was Venetian knowledge as well disseminated as in South Germany. The Turkish ascription of maize suggests further an introduction in the fifteenth or late fourteenth century, prior to which time another Levantine attribution would have been more likely.

The Po Valley long has been known for its large cultivation of maize and for a diet strongly based on dishes prepared from maize. Nowhere in Europe, except to the east of Italy, is maize of comparable importance. Maize growing and eating are similarly characteristic of the Balkans and

Hungary, long and early under Turkish domination. (A study of the origin and meaning of the name *kukuruz* for maize, widely used in Eastern Europe, might be revealing.) The early establishment of maize as a human staple in Venezia, Lombardy, and Emilia, where it is often simply known as "corn" (*formento*) is not to be attributed solely to the advantages of soil and climate, as appears to be true also for the Balkans and Hungary. An early culture historical element also is involved. Edgar Anderson in an article he called Anatolian Mystery (*Landscape,* Spring 1958) has outlined the genetic problem for plants of American origin found in the Near East.

Spain as Intermediary

There is strangely little evidence in support of the theory that maize, pumpkins, paprika, even tobacco, in fact almost any New World plants, were disseminated eastward through the Old World from Spain. Cultivated seed plants originating in the New World are more significant in the eastern end of the Mediterranean and in Italy than they are in Spain, and seem to have been so as far back as there is knowledge of them. Nor are the contacts between Spain and the German lands known to have been productive in plant introductions. Southern areas of German speech and political control came into close relation with Spain through the marriage of Juana and Philip. These contacts were strongest during the long reign of their son Charles V, German emperor and Spanish king. During his reign Spanish soldiers and officials came to Germany in numbers. Persons, posts, and knowledge were in exchange between Spain, Germany, and parts of Italy as at no other time. Witness the role of German printing presses in Spain as well as in Germany in communicating the news of the New World, the employment of German clerks and factors, as by the Welsers and Fuggers, both in Spain and its colonies overseas. Yet in that first half century I know of scarcely any mention of New World plants brought to Central Europe by way of Spain (Tagetes an exception?).

Spanish colonists in the New World did not take readily to native foods if they could provide themselves with the familiar Spanish food items. A familiar illustration is their effort expended to grow wheat in suitable and unsuitable places and the official care to get for every administrative unit a record of all plants "de Castilla" (the so-called *Relaciones Geográficas* from 1579 on). Doctor Francisco Hernández, sent in 1570 by Philip II to make a botano-medical study of the plants of New Spain, wrote concerning *tlaolli* (maize): "I do not understand how the Spaniards, most diligent imitators of what is foreign and who also know so well how to make use of alien inventions, have not as yet adapted to their uses nor have taken to their own country and cultivated this kind of grain," the many admirable qualities of which he then proceeded to set forth. "This aliment," he continued, with reference to New Spain, "is beginning to be liked by Spaniards, but chiefly by those born of Spanish and Indian parents, or of Indian and Negro, or of Negro and Spanish origins." These comments were made late in the sixteenth century and still hold in good part for Spanish America. Maize is for the poor, the Indians, and the mixed breeds, wheat for the better classes in the majority of Hispanic areas. The food of the natives did not find favor with their masters; foodstuffs still mark social status. Columbus brought some maize to Spain, but only here and there, as in remote Galicia adjoining Portugal, did maize become a common food — nor did it do so through the samples brought by Columbus. (The historical geography of maize growing in Spain, for food and for feed remains to be studied.)

Panizo, Columbus, and Peter Martyr

Possibly the oldest name for maize employed in Spain is *panizo*. Neither the name maize, nor any other native name of the New World was popularly adapted early in Spain, Portugal, elsewhere in Europe, or for the most part anywhere in the Old World (except in the Philippines), though the name *mais*, taken from the Island Arawak, came into early use all over Spanish America.

The Journal of the first voyage of Columbus (known through Las Casas' *Historia de las Indias*) under date of November 6, 1492 from the north coast of Cuba, made bare mention of *"panizo"* as cultivated by the natives. On his return to Spain the following spring he brought samples of the grain, which as we shall see, brings Peter Martyr into our theme.

Panizo (Latin *panicum*) is still a provincial name for maize in parts of Spain. According to Corominas[2] "at the discovery of America *panizo,* name of an ancient European grass, became widely applied to maize in many parts of Spain, both of Castilian and Catalan speech." Panicum (common millet, Hirse in German) is about as unlike maize as a grass may be; how the name was transferred from a thin-stalked, small-seeded millet to the robust Indian corn remains unexplained. Nor do I have an idea why Columbus at first called maize panizo. By the time of the first edition of the *Dictionary of the Real Academia Española* (1734–1737) panizo had become just another name for maize.

Columbus gave his account of the discovery overseas to the Court at Barcelona. This took place in May of 1493,

Peter Martyr d'Anghiera being in attendance. The latter, Italian cleric and tutor to the royal princess, had been writing letters on contemporary events to high Roman clergy and Italian nobles. Letter 130 of his *Opus Epistolarum,* written in May 1493, took up the arrival of Columbus at Court. Columbus and his companions, the view of the strange goods and trophies and the appearances of a unknown breed of men of wholly alien culture impressed him strongly and gave new direction thereafter to his life. He was henceforth the great reporter on the new-found world, and seemingly was never taken in by the notion of Columbus, that he had found the Farthest East that Marco Polo had visited. Though Peter Martyr never saw the New World he was perhaps the first to realize that such it was, and he asked the searching questions of the returned voyagers, of high and low degree, to set down the answers in his letters, some of which later were assembled into his *Decades.* We should know a lot less of the newly discovered lands and their life but for the prompt and acute interviews he had with captains, soldiers, clerks, any who came back from overseas. First historian of the New World, he recorded by personal interviews, and he was a most able examiner.

In a letter of September 1493 (no. 133) he noted the dependence of the island natives on root crops as their staples and how they prepared *cazabe* bread; there was still no mention of any grain. Of similar date and content was the next letter (no. 134) to his old friend and patron at Rome, Cardinal Sforza, a fellow Milanese. This was followed by a mid-November letter, also to the Cardinal, in which he wrote:

Panem et ex frumento quodam panico, cuius est apud Insubres et Granatenses hispanos maxima copia, non magno discrimine conficiunt. Est huius panicula longior spithama, in acutum tendens, lacerte fere crassitudine. Grana miro ordine a natura confixa, forma et corpore pisum legumen aemulantur: albent acerba: ubi maturuerunt, nigerrima efficiuntur: fracta candore nivem exuperant: maizium, id frumenti genus appellant. (Decade I, Book I).

It is apparent that Peter Martyr had observed well the maize plants as grown to maturity from seeds brought by Columbus and had recognized the plant. The following spring he wrote once again to Cardinal Sforza (Decade I, Book II) that "the carrier will give you in my name certain white and black seeds of the panicum from which they [the island people] make bread."

Since Peter Martyr wrote in Latin the panizo of Columbus became panicum, but also he set down for the first time the name maiz(ium). The observation is competent and constitutes the earliest description of the plant known: it notes the *panicula,* not the panicle of modern botany, but the ear, in modern Spanish in places still called *panoja.* According to Corominas panoja "lives on in many parts of Spain, in place of mazorca, more favored in common speech"; also Corominas shows its derivation from the classical Latin panicula. After noting that the ear tapered to a point, was longer than the span of one's hand, and almost as thick as the human arm, Peter Martyr described the grains as "affixed by nature in a wondrous manner and in form and size like garden peas, white when young." In both letters he referred to black seeds, in the later one he adds a white-seeded kind. That the color was in the external aleurone layer is indicated by the remark that, broken across, the interior of the seed was whiter than snow.

The plant described differs markedly from the tropical, mostly yellow flint corns of the Caribbean of today. It may be noted that there are agreements in the Peter Martyr, Bock, and Fuchs characterizations of maize.

That bread was made from maize in the West Indies is not mentioned by later writers. Oviedo in his *Natural Historia* of 1526 said that the islanders used maize only toasted (*tostado*, popped??) or as roasting ears in the milk stage. When Oviedo knew the natives they were already advanced in cultural collapse, Peter Martyr on the other hand got his account from the first European contact.

Of highest significance is the identification by Peter Martyr of the grain brought back by Columbus with one which he already knew from two areas of the Mediterranean. Of all grains maize is least likely to be mistaken for something else, unique as it is in its ears, seed, and tassel. The person who wrote the first clear description of maize may not be charged with superficial knowledge. He wrote that this was the grain found in greatest amount among the Insubres and the Spanish of Granada. As one Milanese speaking to another, his old friend the cardinal in Rome, brother of the Duke of Milan, he named their common countrymen as Insubres. The Insubres had been a tribe of Gauls who once had occupied the area about Milan, and the name was a classicism for the people of and about Milan.

Peter Martyr left Milan in 1478 to live in Rome under Sforza patronage. Thence he was called to Spain in 1487. What he wrote the cardinal in 1493 was in effect that this was the same grain with which both of them had been familiar years earlier when they were still living in Milan. He repeated this identification twice in later years. In Book Two of his Eighth Decade he wrote of the maize on the American mainland as like the *panicum* of Lombardy. In Book Two of his Seventh Decade, having interviewed Ayllón and his Indian from the land of Chicora (the Carolinas of southeast United States), he recorded that the bread of Chicora was made of maize as among the islanders and that they lacked cazabi bread: This "maize grain is precisely like (*persimile*) our Insubrian panicum, but is of the size of garden peas."

The other area which Peter Martyr named as having had this grain in cultivation at the return of Columbus was the lately conquered Moorish kingdom of Granada. Again he spoke from personal knowledge for he had been a participant observer throughout that campaign which was carried to its conclusion in 1492.

The testimony of Peter Martyr is entered as that of a key witness, competent and trustworthy, to the effect that maize was cultivated in two parts of the Mediterranean well before the discovery of Columbus.[3]

The Question of Sorghum and Milium

As there has been a transfer of name from the small panic grass to maize, so there has been from Sorghum to maize. (Currently the American farmer is calling a grain sorghum "maize," shortened from "milo maize," itself a term of confusion.) Name without some mention of a diagnostic quality may be misleading, as in the current terms "Guinea corn" and "great millet."

Of the three grains that resemble each other in their tall, stout growth and large strap-like leaves, pearl millet (*Pennisetum glaucum*) probably can be disregarded. Mainly of tropical African and Indian cultivation, there is no evidence that it was present in Europe. A field of young maize may look much like one of sorghum, but the sorghums bear their seed in a terminal inflorescence, panicle, or "brush" that stands conspicuously above the rest of the plant, whereas in maize the seed is enclosed in ears that are set at nodes well below the upper stalk. The ears of maize are wholly distinctive (cf. Peter Martyr's *grana miro ordine confixa*), and the seeds are many times the size of those of sorghums or other millets. Ear and seed readily distinguish maize and sorghum.

Sorghum is much earlier in Europe than maize. The elder Pliny said that within ten years of his writing a *"milium"* had been brought to Italy from India. His description has been accepted by J. D. Snowden, monographer of the *Cultivated Races of Sorghum,* as sufficient to establish the plant as a Sorghum. Milium previously had meant Setaria or Panicum, or both together as millets. Later Roman Sorghum appears to have made slow headway through the Mediterranean, as grain for poultry and as stock feed.

I have gotten very little out of the late medieval writers on agriculture, chief among whom was Pietro de Crescenzi, Italian of the thirteenth century, who was reprinted well into the sixteenth century and was largely copied in Spanish by Gabriel Alonzo de Herrera of Salamanca. Their main concern was with good farming practices. What little they had to say of particular plants, in particular of forage and feed plants, which included the category of "millets," was rarely sufficient to tell which plant was meant. Botanically they were still inclined to repeat the old Greeks and Romans. Classical plant names were applied to right or wrong plants, original observations only casually and scantily introduced. Names derived from milium appear to have referred at least in part to sorghums (such as miglio and melica). Saggina or zahina appear to denote simply fattening feeds.

Sorgo according to Corominas was "already documented

in the Latin form *suricum* in documents of the North of Italy in the thirteenth century" probably meaning "coming from Syria." It is a fair guess therefore that in the later Middle Ages a post-Roman form of Sorghum (which has greatly differing varieties) was introduced from the Levant and acquired some popularity as feed in northern Italy, Venetian trade again serving as intermediary. In Friuli maize is called *sorgo turco* or *sorturco*, the later grain having added the locative word "Turkish" to the older grain that was named from Syria. The earliest use of the name sorgo in the literature of discovery in so far as I know is by Pigafetta during the voyage of Magellan. He identified sorgo as one of the grains in the Philippines. That, as native of Vicenza in the Po Valley, he knew whereof he spoke, is further substantiated by his recording as its native name *"batat,"* which is Malay for sorghum (cf. Malay names in Burkill's *Dictionary of Economic Products of the Malay Peninsula*).

In 1542 Fuchs described and figured a reddish seeded form of Sorghum with very long, lax, panicles as *Sorgi,* or *Welscher Hirse,* saying that it was an alien grain brought to Germany from Italy, was grown in many German gardens, but was of difficult cultivation (climate). Thus he introduced plant and name to the literature of botany. The varieties with dense and stiff panicles, the grain sorghums, such as the durras of African origin and related forms cultivated in the Orient, seem not to have been known in Europe until considerably later times; it is these that mainly are used as human food in dry parts of Africa and Asia.

The origin of the name sorghum thus may be credited to Italy. The name spread north into German lands, but not west into Iberia. Where present in the latter parts, we should expect some variant of milium. A curious note from Peter Martyr is in order here: Puzzling about a grain other than maize reported by his informants from the Carolinas, he says they think it may be "milium", but he was uncertain because very few Castilians know what milium is, "since it is never grown in Castile."

Plural Introductions of Maize into the Iberian Peninsula

Peter Martyr gave positive testimony of maize in Granada prior to Columbus. This may be supported by a Catalan name *blat de moro,* Moorish wheat. Columbus brought maize from the West Indies, and may have given rise to the local name of panizo. Finally throughout Portugal (*milho*) and adjacent Spain (*mijo*), especially in Galicia (*millo*) and on into Gascony (*milhoc*) (Corominas) a name derived from milium was given to maize. This is also true of the Canaries and the Portuguese islands off the African coast. This distribution of milium names down the Atlantic coast requires our attention next.

First, however, a gloss on another name, *borona,* of similar but lesser geographic distribution. Corominas has documented borona in use as far back as 1220 and holds it to be a word of ancient origin, applied to some cereal (a millet?) and the griddlecakes made therefrom to be passed on later to maize "bread" and maize. The accounts of the Spanish occupation of the Philippines in and after 1566 refer occasionally to borona, perhaps to a millet like the one known in Spain. Distribution and meaning of this name need study. In Portuguese both at home and overseas milho, with or without a qualifying word, is the standard or only word for maize and was so from early days.

Milho and Zaburro

Pigafetta, Italian chronicler of the voyage of Magellan, noted about Rio de Janeiro that the Indians were growing *miglio* (Italian spelling, same pronunciation as the Portuguese milho). The crew was partly Spanish, and from some who had been in the Caribbean he learned that there it was called *"mais."* As miglio the grain was familiar, the new thing was that it had an Indian name.

In the Vizayan part of the Philippine Islands Pigafetta noted miglio/millio repeatedly. This may be entered as the first records of maize in the Philippines, antedating by a half century the introduction from New Spain. Pigafetta may be accepted as knowing what he saw. He was not only generally a good observer, but (1) he had been correct in Brazil in identifying miglio with maize, (2) he recognized sorghum when he saw it in the Philippines, as was cited above, (3) when forced tribute was levied on the Vizayan natives these were required to bring equal quantities of rice and miglio, rice and maize being most desirable and familiar as ship stores to those who had sailed African shores.

These early milho/maize terms from Brazil and the Philippines lead us to the Portuguese on the coasts of Africa and their early knowledge of maize. This subject has long been the special concern of Professor M. D. W. Jeffreys of the University of Witwatersrand.[4] I thought to have a look on my own through the early Portuguese writings on overseas and found the Jeffreys thesis confirmed that maize in Africa was pre-Columbian and that the Portuguese took it to Portugal from Africa, not from America.

Soares de Souza wrote a detailed and competent description of the natural history and geography of northeastern Brazil in the second half of the sixteenth century, *Grandeza de Bahia de Todos os Santos.* He came to Brazil a generation after its first colonization, but had long and intimate knowledge of the colony and a special interest in the cultivated plants. He described the maize plant and its uses, noting that there were white, ochreous, black- and red-seeded races and also a soft-seeded (flour) form, adding "the Indians [Tupi] call ubatim [abatí] what is the *milho de Guiné*, which in Portugal they call *zaburro*." Maize in his time was the staple food of the Negro slaves on the plantations. Guinea corn and zaburro he recognized as synonyms for milho (maize).

João de Barros in his Historia of the mid-sixteenth century described the Jalofa (Wolof) Negroes living between the Senegal and Gambia rivers, as practicing a peculiar manner of sowing *"millios de maçaroca a que chamamos zaburro"* (the cob-bearing milho which we call zaburro). This "was the common sustenance of these peoples." Ramusio added to his Italian version the marginal comment "the maize of the western Indies, on which half the world is nourished and which the Portuguese call miglio zaburro."

About the year 1530 an anonymous Portuguese pilot wrote about navigation from Lisbon to the Island of São Tomé in the Gulf of Guinea, telling of "the grain which is called *miglio Zaburro* and in the western Indies is called maize, of the size of chick peas and common to all the [Cape Verde] islands and all the coast of Africa and upon which the inhabitants sustain themselves." It was made into bread "which then was sold throughout the coast of Africa, or land of the Negroes, and was traded for black slaves." It was also grown on the lately colonized island of São Tomé for and by Negro slaves who had been brought from the near mainland.[5]

The Portuguese crown sent a mission to seek out Prester

John in 1515; it traveled through Ethiopia from 1520 to 1526 and returned home in 1527.[6] In this account I found reference at seven localities to milho or milho zaburro, such as meeting cattle people, very black, naked, and claiming to be Christians, who were guarding their fields sown to milho zaburro and had come from afar to sow it on very high and steep mountainsides (ch. 8), of bread made from a mixture of milho zaburro, barley and a small black seed called tafa [Eragrostis teff] (ch. 13), of traveling through canes of milho as thick as those used in staking grapes (ch. 33), of passing through *milharadas* as tall as sugar cane (ch. 49).

A German in Portuguese services, known as Valentim Fernandes, has left an early and informative account of African coasts as known before 1508.[7] About Quyloa (Kilwa in southern Tanganyika) there was much *milho* like that of Guinea, all the gardens surrounded with wooden stakes and canes of milho like *canaveaes* (sugar cane fields), the stalks as tall as a man (pp. 14–16). The Gyloffa (Wolof of Senegal), as Barros again described them later, had much *milho zaburro,* and as their chief food *cuscus* made of milho zaburro, their manner of grinding and baking same being described (pp. 67ff.). The Mandingo, southern neighbors of the Wolof, consumed much rice and milho zaburro. Of São Tomé Fernandes wrote that milho zaburro began to be planted there in 1502, about ten years after its colonization, this grain having previously been brought in by ship from mainland Guinea. An important sentence explains the nature of this milho zaburro: *"E nace propio como ho daca se non q nace grande e o milho en hua maça e non espalhado como o nosso"* (p. 128): "It grows like ours, except that it grows large with the seeds in one mass and not spread apart like ours." This is a good comparison of maize and sorghum, the massive ear as against the lax panicle of the sorghum then known in Europe (cf. the plate of *Sorgi* in Fuchs). Also this is the nearest approximation we have to a time when maize was not yet established in Portugal, for the milho of Portugal to which he compares the milho zaburro was certainly not maize.

Milho has long since become the common name for maize in Portuguese, but zaburro also continues to be its name, or the name of a variety.[8] Milho zaburro seems to have been the earliest Portuguese name for maize and the name came out of the Guinea Coast. It was in use years before the Portuguese colonization of Brazil began. Milho de Guiné became a Portuguese name for maize in Brazil and elsewhere, to be applied in error in later years, especially in the English "Guinea corn," to sorghum. (Cf. The Spanish Main, in Spanish the Tierra Firme of Continental America, which was transferred in English usage to become the name of the Caribbean Sea.) Jeffreys makes a telling point, saying that in twenty years of residence on the Guinea coast he never saw sorghum grown there, nor is it at all climatically suited to the tropical rain forest; the sorghums belong to the dry African margins.

The origin of the name zaburro and of its appearance on the Guinea coast I must leave to Jeffreys and others who know African languages and early history. Dalziel in his *Flora of Tropical Africa* supports Jeffreys as to zaburro/maize names for tribes of the Gold Coast and Dahomey. (In reading Dalziel I wondered whether there might be a connection with the *Digitaria Iburua* cultivated as a grain, as by Hausa tribes in Northern Nigeria.) Jeffreys is of the opinion that maize was communicated by Arab contacts and pressures out of the north and northeast in the late Middle

Ages. He may well be right and if so there may be a common source for Guinea and Turkish corn.

The identification of milho as maize, which the Portuguese first learned to know on the Guinea Coast, throws some light on the African slave trade. Maize "bread" from the coast was used for trading in slaves (food shortage in the interior?). Maize was shipped to the African islands to feed the slaves until the islands grew their own supply. Maize was the staple food of the African slaves in Brazil. The inference is that maize was taken with the Negro slaves wherever the Portuguese went, to Brazil and to Portugal. It was available on the coast of Guinea, the leading source of slaves; it was accustomed food of the coastal Negroes; it was more readily transported than yams and other roots; it was a main food crop on the sugar plantations. It may be therefore that some of the older maize varieties grown in Brazil were introduced from Africa.

Notes from Leo Africanus

Leo Africanus, the Moorish house slave of the Medici Pope Leo X, may have something to add for the Sudan. Born in Granada he was taken to Morocco when the Kingdom of Granada fell to the Spanish arms in 1492. In early manhood he traveled widely about North Africa, crossing the Sahara into the Sudan. These southern travels are dated around 1514; his capture, sale, and coming into the hands of the Pope between 1518 and 1520. As the letters of Peter Martyr informed the Pope about the New World, so the Moorish captive was prevailed upon to write or indite a geographic handbook of Mohammedan Africa.

The Seventh Part of Leo's Description of Africa dealt, somewhat briefly, with the Land of the Negroes, by which he meant peoples more or less converted to Islam and living about the Middle Niger, both to the west and east of Timbuktu. His knowledge barely extended to forest Negroes farther south, and not at all to the Guinea Coast. For the "kingdom" of Gualata (Oualata, in the edge of the desert to the west of Timbuktu) he said there was "little grain and this is miglio (here probably durra Sorghum) and another sort of grain, round and white like *cece* (Cicer, chickpeas) which is not seen in Europe." Far to the southeast of Timbuktu, in Guber (Gober, a district in the new Republic of Niger) Leo observed "a great quantity of miglio and rice and another grain which I have not seen in Italy, but believe that such is to be found in Spain."

In Sudanese lands, where durra has long been a staple as well as rice where the local situation was favorable, he noted at two widely distant localities "another grain," which may well have been maize. The seeds, and the only noted grain, were round, white, and large like chick peas. Only maize fits these characteristics; comparison to chickpeas has been noted above in Portuguese accounts. He had not seen such a grain in Italy, but he did not know Lombardy or Venezia and he had limited occasion to travel in Italy. He thought the "other grain" of Guber was to be found in Spain; Peter Martyr had said that maize was grown in Granada, the birthplace of Leo, at the time of the conquest.

Conclusion

This study has been based in the main on printed documents of the time of the Great Discoveries. None of them supports the notion that Columbus was first to bring maize to Europe, nor that it came to be disseminated to other parts of the Old World by way of Spain and Portugal. Nor do I know evidence for such dramatically rapid spread of this grain as Laufer inferred in his view of its carriage by land in a few decades from Spain east to China. A new food plant finds its way more gradually into an economy. The grower must learn how to plant, cultivate, harvest and store it, how to fit it into his cropping practices, and how to meet its requirements of weather and soil; the housewife needs to learn how to prepare it in dishes that gain acceptance. Such learning and change of habit take time. At what times and by what routes maize was carried into the Old World still remains to be determined in large part. Its entry into Europe is indicated as pre-Columbian (Balkans, Italy, and Granada), Columbian, and post-Columbian (milho into Portugal out of Guinea). Further light may be expected from documents (Turkish tax lists, Arab travels, accounts of Venetian and Portuguese trade), vernacular names for maize, and perhaps most of all from the phylogenetic study of old local races of maize that survive in Europe, Africa, and Asia.

NOTES ON "MAIZE INTO EUROPE"

[1] E. Stuler: Leonard Fuchs, Munich, 1928, p. 231.

[2] J. Corominas: Diccionario Crítico Etimológico de la Lengua Castellana, four volumes (Madrid, 1954).

[3] Edgar Anderson has called my attention to the Notebooks of Leonardo da Vinci for two references to maize. I have seen only the one-volume edition and translation by Edward MacCurdy (1939). Discussing the liver, Leonardo makes a comparison with "maize or Indian millet, when their grains have been separated" (p. 116). In the Miscellany (p. 1184) there is mention of "beans, white maize, red maize, panic-grass, millet, kidney beans, broad beans, peas." The jottings are thought to have begun in 1508; Leonardo died in 1519.

[4] A late exposition by him is "Origin of the Portuguese Word Zaburro" in *Bull. de l'Institut Français d'Afrique Noire*, Vol. XIX.

[5] G. Ramusio, *Navigatione e Viaggi*, Vol. 1, pp. 125–28.

[6] P. Frco. Alvares: Verdadera Informaçáon das Terras do Preste João.

[7] O Manuscrito "Valentim Fernandes," *Acad. Port. Hist.*, 1941.

[8] The custodian of our quarters at the University, Antonio Trindade, native of Madeira, when asked what zaburro was, answered that it is corn of large purplish black seeds, which are white inside.

[167]

Index

[170]

[172]